THE AMERICAN BAR ASSOCIATION

GUIDE TO
WILLS AND
ESTATES

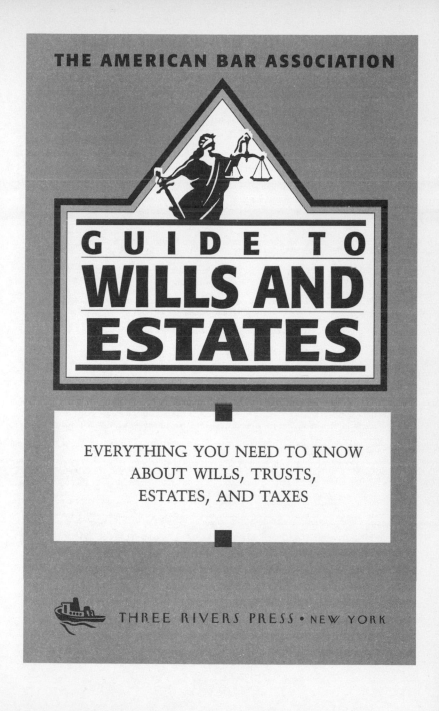

THE AMERICAN BAR ASSOCIATION

GUIDE TO
WILLS AND
ESTATES

EVERYTHING YOU NEED TO KNOW
ABOUT WILLS, TRUSTS,
ESTATES, AND TAXES

THREE RIVERS PRESS • NEW YORK

Published by Three Rivers Press, New York, New York.
Member of the Crown Publishing Group.

Random House, Inc. New York, Toronto, London, Sydney, Auckland
www.randomhouse.com

THREE RIVERS PRESS and the Tugboat design are registered trademarks of Random House, Inc.

Originally published by Times Books in 1995.

Printed in the United States of America

Library of Congress Cataloging-in-Publication Data
The American Bar Association guide to wills and estates / by the American Bar Association—1st ed.
    Includes index.
    1. Wills—United States—Popular works. 2. Trusts and trustees—United States—Popular works. 3. Estate planning—United States—Popular works. I. American Bar Association.
KF755.Z9A376   1995
346.7305'2—dc20
[347.30652]   95-2489

ISBN 0-8129-2536-X
10

The updates to this book are by Lena S. Barnett. Ms. Barnett is an estate planning attorney in private practice in Silver Spring, Maryland. She is one of the original contributing reviewers of this book. Ms. Barnett has served as a vice chair of the Probate, Trust & Estate Planning Committee of the General Practice Section of the American Bar Association and as chair of the Estates and Trusts Section of the Bar Association of Montgomery County, Maryland. She is a fellow of the Esperti Peterson Institute for Wealth Strategies Planning.

FOREWORD

■

HILARIE BASS, *Chair*
ABA Standing Committee on Public Education

THE LAW AFFECTS each of us in our daily lives—when we send our kids to school, take the car in for repair, use a credit card, make a purchase, or go to work. If we don't understand how law governs our rights and responsibilities, we're at a considerable disadvantage in today's America.

That is the purpose of *The American Bar Association Legal Guides*—to explain the law to you in simple, easy-to-understand language. These books are concise and straightforward. By avoiding legal jargon and technicalities, they discuss in everyday words how the law affects you at home, at work, and at play. Best of all, these books will help you to avoid legal problems, to identify those that you may have, and to determine which legal problems you can solve on your own and which require the assistance of an attorney.

These books help you understand the important legal issues about marriage, separation, and divorce. They explore the legal aspects of owning a home, and the world of contracts, big and little. They tell you what you need to know to plan your estate *and* save money for yourself and your loved ones. They even provide guidance on planning for disability, and on end-of-life issues.

These books are organized so you can easily find what you need to know. Brief articles giving additional information on topics of great interest appear alongside the text. You will also find information about state laws, as well as about federal laws that apply across the United States.

No book can answer all the questions you might have on the law. To help you find additional help, sections at the end of each book tell you where to get more information. These sections refer you to many free or inexpensive publications, and suggest services that government agencies, bar associations, and other groups can provide at either minimal or no cost.

When reading *The American Bar Association Legal Guides*, please keep some important points in mind. First, these books cannot and do not pretend to provide legal advice—only a lawyer who understands the facts of your particular case can do that. Although every effort has been made to present material that is as up-to-date as possible, laws can and do change.

Thus, these books should be considered an introduction to the law in each area. They are not the final word. If you are thinking about pursuing any legal action, consult first with a lawyer, bar association, or lawyer referral service to assure yourself of knowledgeable assistance. Armed with the knowledge and insights provided in *The American Bar Association Legal Guides*, you can be confident that the legal decisions you make will be in your best interests.

Hilarie Bass is in private practice in Miami, Florida. She is president of the Florida Bar Foundation and a past member of the Board of Governors of the American Bar Association.

AMERICAN BAR ASSOCIATION

■

Robert A. Stein,
Executive Director

Mabel C. McKinney-Browning,
Director, Division for Public Education

Charles White,
Series Editor

Allan Bogutz
Bogutz & Gordon, P.C.
Tucson, Arizona

Alexander J. Bott
University of North Dakota
  School of Law
Grand Forks, North Dakota

Charles A. Collier, Jr.
Irell & Manella
Los Angeles, California

Edgar T. Farmer
Ziercher & Hocker
St. Louis, Missouri

Max Gutierrez, Jr.
Brobeck, Phleger & Harrison
San Francisco, California

William D. Haught
Attorney at Law
Little Rock, Arkansas

J. Rodney Johnson
University of Richmond, the
  T. C. Williams School of Law
Richmond, Virginia

Jerry Frank Jones
Owen, Jones, Bogart & Rogers
Elgin, Texas

Mildred Kalik
Simpson, Thacher & Bartlett
New York, New York

Jeffrey B. Kolb
Emison, Doolittle, Kolb &
  Roellgen
Vincennes, Indiana

Clifton B. Kruse, Jr.
Kruse & Lynch, P.C.
Colorado Springs, Colorado

Richard A. Leigh
Trickel, Leigh & Mann, P.A.
Orlando, Florida

William Sitzer
Dubail Judge
St. Louis, Missouri

Susan S. Westerman
Attorney at Law
Ann Arbor, Michigan

PREFACE

■

ROBERT A. STEIN, *Executive Director*
American Bar Association

THE AMERICAN BAR ASSOCIATION legal guides are designed to provide guidance for people on important legal questions they encounter in everyday life. When American families are asked to describe their legal needs, the topics that come up repeatedly are housing, personal finance, family and domestic concerns (usually in conjunction with divorce and child support), wills and estates, and employment-related issues. In addition, more and more Americans have questions about operating a business, often out of the home.

These are the topics that *The American Bar Association Legal Guides* cover in plain, direct language. We have made a special effort to make the books practical, by using situations and problems you are likely to encounter. The goal of these books is to give helpful information on a range of options that can be used in solving everyday legal problems, so that you can make informed decisions on how best to handle your particular question.

The American Bar Association wants Americans to be aware of the full range of options available when they are confronted with a problem that might have a "legal" solution. The Association has supported programs to eliminate delay in the courts, and has worked to promote fast, affordable alternatives to lawsuits, such as mediation, arbitration, conciliation, and small claims court. Through ABA support for lawyer referral programs and pro bono services (where lawyers donate their time), people have been able to find the best lawyer for their particular case and have received quality legal help within their budget.

The American Bar Association Legal Guides discuss all these alternatives, suggesting the wide range of options open to you. We hope that they will help you feel more comfortable with the law and will remove much of the mystery from the legal system.

Several hundred members of the Association have contributed to *The American Bar Association Legal Guides*—as authors and as reviewers who have guaranteed the guides' accuracy. To them—and to the ABA's Standing Committee on Public Education, which was the primary force behind the publications—I express my thanks and gratitude, and that of the Association and of lawyers everywhere.

Robert A. Stein is executive director of the American Bar Association. He was formerly dean of the University of Minnesota Law School.

PREFACE

CONTENTS

THE AMERICAN BAR ASSOCIATION

GUIDE TO
WILLS AND
ESTATES

CHAPTER ONE

■

Getting Started

ESTATE PLANNING. The phrase sounds so dry, distant, and foreboding. It's unfortunate that so many people shy away from even the thought of it, because planning your estate is really about caring for your loved ones, seeing that they are provided for, and making sure that your hard-earned property is distributed according to your wishes.

Your estate consists of all your property, including:

- your home and other real estate;

- **tangible personal property**, such as cars and furniture; and

- **intangible property**, such as insurance, bank accounts, stocks and bonds, and pension and Social Security benefits.

An estate plan is your blueprint for managing your estate while you are alive and upon your disability, and providing for where you want your property to go after you die.

While a will is usually the most important part of an estate plan, it's not the only part. These days, it's common for a person to have a dozen "will substitutes"—that is, various ways of distributing property regardless of whether the person has a formal will. Pensions, gifts, joint ownership, and trusts are but a few of the ways you can transfer property during your lifetime or at death both quickly and inexpensively. Many devices like life insurance and bank accounts with right of survivorship are set up to take effect at death.

Not Just for the Elderly

We're all squeamish about death, but, increasingly, we're over-coming our reluctance to plan for it. The number of Americans with wills, for example, has grown by 50 percent in just fifteen years. Thanks in part to growing interest in living wills, simplified procedures, and lower costs, millions of people of all ages and economic levels have taken steps to distribute their money and property according to a sound estate plan.

Estate planning is emphatically not just for the elderly. One glance at the news demonstrates that far too many young and middle-aged people die suddenly, often leaving behind children who need care and direction. Estate planning needs to be factored into your overall financial plan, along with providing for your children's college tuition and your own retirement needs. If your financial or family circumstances change later in life, it's usually easy and inexpensive to adjust your plan.

Most people also plan for mental or physical incapacity resulting from an accident or illness. Through living wills, health-care powers of attorney, and other mechanisms, they control beforehand how they and their property are to be cared for if disaster strikes.

The Law of Intestacy

If you die **intestate** (without a will), your property must still be distributed. By not leaving a valid will or trust, or transferring your property in some other way (such as through insurance, pension benefits, or joint ownership), you've in effect left it to state law to write your will for you. This doesn't mean that your money will go to the state—that only happens in the very rare cases where there are no surviving relatives, even very remote ones. It does mean, however, that the state will make certain assumptions about where you'd like your money to go—assumptions with which you might not agree. Intestate descent laws prefer "blood" over "marriage," assuming—perhaps wrongly—that the more closely related you are to someone, the more likely it is that you'd want your property to go to him or her. Some of your hard-earned money might end up with people who don't need it—for example, your grown child who already has more than you. Meanwhile, others who do need the money or are more deserving—such as that favorite niece of yours, or your other child who has had trouble finding steady work—could be short-changed. Surviving relatives may squabble over who gets particular items of your property, since you didn't make these decisions before you died.

Intestacy laws might also fail to provide adequate support for your spouse. For example, if you leave a spouse and no children, in many states your spouse shares with your parents if they're alive, and he or she may get as little as half of your property. Under the laws of some states, if there are sufficient assets, your spouse would get a sum set by law—perhaps $5,000, $10,000, or $25,000, depending on the state, plus half the balance; your parents would get the rest. Some states simply require your spouse and parents to split fifty-fifty. Most people want the spouse to get all the property, but if they don't leave a will that probably won't happen. The way to ensure that it will happen, and that your other goals will be achieved, is to plan your estate. Only estate planning gives you the feeling of control that comes from knowing your family is provided for as you wish. You decide who gets your property, when they get it, how they get it, and how much they get. Estate planning makes you the boss.

TEN THINGS ESTATE PLANNING CAN DO FOR YOU

The first step in planning your estate is to identify your major objectives. Here are some typical objectives, preliminary suggestions on meeting them, and a guide to the chapters in this book that discuss your options in more detail.

1. Provide for your immediate family. Couples want to provide enough money for the surviving spouse. They often choose to provide this income through life insurance, particularly for spouses who don't work outside of the home.

Couples with children want to assure their education and upbringing. If you have children under eighteen, both you and your spouse should have a will nominating **personal guardians for the children**, in case you both should die before they grow up. Otherwise, a court will decide without your input where your kids will live and who will make important decisions about their money, education, and way of life. (See chapter 6.)

2. Provide for other relatives who need help and guidance. Do you have family members whose lives might become more difficult without you, such as an elderly parent or disabled child, or a grandchild whose education you want to assure? You could establish a special **trust fund** for family members who need support that you won't be there to provide. (See chapter 4.)

3. Get your property to beneficiaries quickly. You want your beneficiaries to receive promptly the property you've left them. Options include avoiding or greatly easing **probate** (the court process for distributing assets left in a will) through insurance paid directly to beneficiaries, **joint tenancy**, a **living trust**, or other means (see chapters 2 and 5); using **simplified** or **expedited probate**, which is available in all states, though sometimes only for very small estates or if all beneficiaries agree (see chapter 11); and taking advantage of laws in certain states that provide partial payments to beneficiaries while a will is in probate (see chapter 11).

4. Plan for incapacity. During estate planning, most people these days also plan for possible mental or physical incapacity. This planning is especially important for single people. **Living wills** and **durable health-care powers of attorney** enable you to decide in advance about life support and pick someone to make decisions for you about medical treatment (see chapter 12). Florida and a number of other states now permit you to designate a **personal guardian**. In addition, disability insurance can protect you and your family if you should become disabled and unable to work.

5. Minimize expenses. Everyone wants to keep the cost of transferring property to beneficiaries as low as possible, which leaves more money for the beneficiaries. Good estate planning can reduce these expenses significantly. (See the final sections of this chapter and chapters 2 through 5.)

6. Choose executors/trustees for your estate. Your **executor** will be responsible for carrying out the directions you express in your will. A **trustee** carries out the directions contained in a trust. Choosing a competent executor and trustee and giving them clear directions is essential to your estate plan. (See chapter 10.)

7. Ease the strain on your family. Many people take a burden from their grieving survivors and also plan their funeral arrangements when planning their estate (see chapter 11).

8. Help a favorite cause. Your estate plan can help support religious, educational, and other charitable causes, either during your lifetime or upon your death, and at the same time take advantage of tax laws designed to encourage private philanthropy (see chapter 8).

9. Reduce taxes on your estate. Every dollar your estate has to pay in estate or inheritance taxes is a dollar that your beneficiaries won't get. A good estate plan can give the maximum allowed by law to your beneficiaries and the minimum to the government. This becomes especially important if your estate is nearly $1 million, since with appreciation it might then approach the level at which the federal estate tax kicks in. (See chapter 8.)

10. Make sure your business goes on smoothly. If you have a business, the operation might be thrown into chaos upon your disability or death. You can provide for an orderly succession and continuation of its affairs by spelling out what will happen to your interest in the business. (See chapter 7.)

TAKING INVENTORY

Once you've established your general objectives, it's time to get specific. Make up a checklist of assets and debts—what you own and what you owe. Below is a list of important estate-planning documents that will provide a good idea of what you'll need to consider. You may also want to complete the more extensive "Estate Planning Checklist" in Appendix A. It is detailed enough to be useful if you have a large, diversified estate, and is equally helpful if yours is a smaller, simpler estate. It will also enable you to do much of the preliminary work needed to prepare a solid estate plan.

Estate Planning Information

In planning your estate, it's helpful to have as much of the following information on hand as possible.

• The names, addresses, and birth dates of your spouse, children, and other relatives whom you might want to include in your will. List any disabilities or other special needs they may have.

• The names, addresses, and phone numbers of possible guardians (if you have young children) and executors or trustees.

• The amount and sources of your income, including interest, dividends, and other household income, such as your spouse's salary or income your children bring home, if they live with you.

• The amounts and sources of all your debts, including mortgages, installment loans, leases, and business debts.

• The amounts and sources of any retirement benefits, including IRAs, pensions, Keogh accounts, government benefits, and profit-sharing plans.

• The amounts, sources, and account numbers of other financial assets, including bank accounts, annuities, outstanding loans, etc.

• A list of life insurance policies, including the account balances, companies' names and addresses, owners, beneficiaries, and any amounts borrowed against the policies.

• A list (with approximate worth) of valuable property you own, including real estate, jewelry, furniture, jointly owned property (name the co-owner), collections, heirlooms, and other assets. This list could be cross-referenced with the names of the people you might want to leave each item to.

• Any documents that might affect your estate plan, including prenuptial agreements, marriage certificates, divorce decrees, recent tax returns, existing wills and trusts, property deeds, etc.

WHO CAN HELP AND WHAT IT WILL COST

If your estate is relatively small and your objectives are not complicated, you might plan your estate mostly on your own, with the help of this book and other resource materials, and seek professional help mostly for tasks like writing a will or trust. Planning for larger estates can involve the counsel of your lawyer, insurance adviser, accountant, and banker, as well as family and friends.

For a basic will or living trust, your lawyer will likely charge a flat fee that covers the costs of consulting with you, drawing up and executing the document, and any required filing fees. These days, most people need more than just a will, so many lawyers offer a package of estate-planning documents, including a basic will, a living will, and durable health-care power of attorney.

A SPECIAL NOTE FOR SPOUSES

You can't plan your estate if you don't know the facts about all the family assets. Yet even in this era, lawyers say they still find that many clients who come to them for estate-planning advice don't have basic information about their spouse's income. All too often, the client doesn't know how much the spouse earns, what benefits he or she is entitled to, or where the money is invested. Whatever the reason for this situation, you need to know this information when planning your estate. It's especially important to find out how property you and your spouse own is titled, including insurance and other beneficiary designations.

Many people might be afraid to cause a rift in the marriage by asking a spouse about financial affairs—especially if that spouse is the primary breadwinner in the family. The need to share information and plan ahead can be raised indirectly—through another family member, an attorney, or other trusted professional—but full knowledge of the family's assets should be part of any sound estate plan.

More extensive estates, particularly those nearing $1 million, generally require professional help in minimizing taxes. More complex estates may involve one or more trusts in addition to a will.

With extensive estates, the lawyer often charges by the hour for the amount of work put into the estate plan. Ask about such fees at your first consultation and inquire about how much your total estate plan might cost. If you use a lawyer who charges by the hour, the more work you do in putting your wishes and the details of your estate in writing, the less work your lawyer has to do and the lower the fee.

Preparing a Will or Trust

Even if you've done a lot of thinking about your estate plan on your own, don't just expect to pile some papers on your lawyer's desk and have a will or trust magically appear in a few weeks. Preparing these documents is seldom as simple as filling in blanks on a form. Most people will meet with their lawyer several times in the process, with more complicated estates requiring more consultations.

CHOOSING A LAWYER

How do you find a lawyer to help you plan your estate and write any necessary documents? You can ask friends who have hired lawyers to draw up their wills, or you can call your local bar association's lawyer referral program, which may list lawyers who specialize in estate practice. You can also write to the American College of Trust and Estate Counsel, 3415 S. Sepulveda Blvd., Suite 330, Los Angeles, CA 90034 for the name of a lawyer in your community. Lawyers will often offer a first consultation free of charge. At this get-acquainted session, you can ask about the lawyer's experience in estate planning and get a firm idea of fees.

An essential: Be comfortable with the lawyer you choose! A good estate lawyer will have to ask questions about many private matters, and you need to feel free in discussing these personal considerations with him or her. If you don't feel comfortable, find another lawyer who's willing to explain the options to you and who'll help you do it right.

At the first meeting, you would probably discuss your financial situation and estate-planning goals. Be prepared to tell your lawyer about intimate details of your life: how much money you have, how many more children you plan to have, which relatives you want to get more (or less) of your assets. Your lawyer will review any documents you've brought in and ask questions that will help you think through various issues and possibilities. Then, he or she will probably outline some of the options the law provides for accomplishing your goals. Though certain methods may be recommended over others, depending on your circumstances, it will still be up to you to make your own choices from among those options.

Then, based on the choices you have made, your lawyer will draft a will or trust or both. At a second meeting, he or she will review that document with you. If it meets with your approval, it can be signed then and there.

For more complicated estates, you may have some long phone conversations or meetings with your lawyer and perhaps have to review several drafts of various estate-planning documents before everything is settled.

You should review your estate plan periodically (see chapter 9), so you'll want to stay in touch with your lawyer. Don't think of estate planning as a onetime transaction but as an occasional process that works best when you have a continuing relationship with your professional advisers.

Other Costs

Good estate planning, as described above, should minimize costs that come about after your death. These include the following:

- **Probate costs. Probate** is the court-supervised legal procedure that (1) determines the validity of your will and (2) gathers and distributes your assets. As chapter 11 details, the expenses of probate vary according to the state, since the requirements for simplified or expedited probate vary considerably. Good estate planning can minimize these expenses by passing assets through legal devices other than a will, thus limiting the size of your **probate estate**. The smaller the estate, the lower the costs, especially if it is small enough to qualify for quick and inexpensive processing.

- **Executor's fees.** By having a will and planning well, you can minimize the executor's fees. If you name a relative who's a beneficiary under the will as executor (most likely your spouse or an adult child), he or she will probably waive the fee. On the other hand, if you die without a will, the probate court will appoint a **personal representative** (usually a family member) to see the estate through probate, most likely at a cost to be deducted from your estate. Similarly, if you pick a third party such as a lawyer to be the executor, he or she is entitled to a "reasonable fee" for seeing an uncontested will through probate.

- **Legal fees in probate.** If your estate is small and uncomplicated and your will is well drafted, your spouse or other executor may be able to reduce the costs of administration. If things get more complex—for example, someone challenges the will, the will is out-of-date because you have a new spouse or child, the will is improperly prepared or executed, etc.—the cost of legal services

A FAMILY MEETING

Of course, a couple should communicate with each other so they agree on what goes to the surviving spouse and what to the children.

Because estate planning affects several generations, it may be a good idea, especially for families with grown children, to make your plan a family affair. Some families set aside a day and gather all the members who are involved. The parents can explain how this plan can have a major influence on all their lives and why they're distributing gifts and trusts the way they are. They can also find out whether the children want to continue the family business and ask if any property has sentimental value to them.

If you have such a meeting, encourage your family to voice their concerns and feelings about all this—remember, many people don't like to talk about death—and answer any questions they may have. (This is especially important when personal or financial considerations lead you to make unequal distributions among siblings; fairness doesn't always mean equal treatment, and you need to spell out the good reasons for making unequal arrangements to avoid later resentment.) They may even raise issues that will lead you to call your lawyer or change your estate plan.

On the other hand, while you should listen to constructive suggestions you needn't be defensive about the informed choices you make. Remember that you don't owe your children anything after they're grown up and that you have the right to enjoy some or all of what you've earned. This meeting can be a chance to make that clear but also to address any insecurities (possibly overwrought) that these decisions may inspire.

becomes greater. You should count on paying whatever the going hourly rate is for a lawyer in your area. The more complex the probate process, the more hours the lawyer will have to put in—and the more it will cost your survivors.

HOW THIS BOOK CAN HELP

In this book, we'll acquaint you with the basics of estate planning—wills, trusts, living wills, and other ways of planning for your death or disability. Our goal is to help you devise the best estate plan by making you an informed consumer.

This guidebook can help you make decisions about writing a will, setting up a trust, using a lawyer or other professional adviser, and other matters involved in planning your estate. Remember that much of the law in this area varies according to the state in which you live or where the property is located, so not all the information provided here will necessarily apply to you. But even in such cases, you will learn what issues to consider, questions to ask, pitfalls to avoid, and where to turn for information and assistance.

This book will help you save money by pointing out how the preparation you do—and even your willingness to do some simple administrative tasks yourself—can cut down on your lawyer's time and thus on your legal bills. You'll also get better service by being prepared and knowledgeable, and by asking the right questions. With this book's help, you should be able to ensure that you receive an estate plan tailored to fit your needs.

Finally, a note on legal terms. The law has its own language, and though this is a book for nonlawyers, we're occasionally forced to use some technical terms or words to which the law assigns special meanings that may not always match our everyday usage. We'll define such terms as we go along.

CHAPTER TWO

■

Transferring Property Without a Will

A Cautionary Tale

DARREN AND SAMANTHA are newlyweds, each of whom has grown children from a previous marriage. They decide to buy a house together and take title to it in **joint tenancy with right of survivorship**, making them co-owners.

After unpacking the last boxes, the happy couple decide to complete the remaking of their lives and rewrite their wills. Both of them want their assets to go to their own children from their first marriages. So each writes a basic will that leaves everything he or she had before the marriage to his or her own children. Samantha's daughter, Tabitha, who is living in a tiny apartment with her husband and kids, will get Darren and Samantha's house when Samantha dies; Darren's children, who have nice homes already, will get the rest of the couple's assets. And a few years later Samantha dies, content because she believes she has provided for her daughter and her family.

Samantha will never know that her estate plan failed to accomplish the one thing she wanted most: giving her house to her daughter. She didn't realize that the joint tenancy she and Darren created meant that ownership of the entire house passed to Darren at the moment of her death regardless of what her will said. She never knew that Darren was later beset by several costly illnesses and had to sell the house. *His* children—not hers—received what was left when Darren died two years later. A **prenuptial agreement** (a signed contract between Darren and

Samantha before their marriage) or a **postnuptial agreement** (signed by them after their marriage) would have prevented this. It also could have been prevented by putting the house only in Samantha's name, or by Samantha and Tabitha holding it in joint ownership with right of survivorship.

Unfortunately, this situation is familiar to many estate lawyers. Too many people don't understand that there's more to estate planning than writing a will. A will cannot change the legal effect of most other devices.

A will is usually the most important document in planning your estate, but it doesn't cover everything. In the **community property** states (see "Community Property," pages 21–22), your will can only control half of most marital assets. Other benefits not controlled by a will or trust include IRAs, insurance policies, income savings plans, retirement plans, and joint tenancy (some jurisdictions also have a special form of joint tenancy for married couples called **tenancy by the entireties**). A good estate plan must coordinate all of these benefits and assets with your will and trust. Using them well can give your beneficiaries money much more efficiently than a will can. Using them badly, like Samantha, can negate your estate plan and frustrate your wishes.

Let's look briefly at the other ways you can transfer property.

Retirement Benefits and Annuities: Beyond the Gold Watch

Most of us are entitled to retirement benefits from an employer. Typically, a retirement plan will pay benefits to beneficiaries if you die before reaching retirement age. After retirement, you can usually pick an option that will continue payments to a beneficiary after your death.

In most cases, the law requires that some portion of these retirement benefits be paid to your spouse. These may be rejected only with your spouse's properly witnessed, signed consent. (These accounts are subject to the payment of the income tax that has been deferred during their existence. Sometimes a spouse rejects benefits because of tax consequences or because there is enough income from other sources and the money might be better used by another beneficiary; check your plan to see what is

PROPERTY THAT DOES NOT PASS VIA A WILL

- *Property held in joint tenancy.*
- *Life insurance payable to a named beneficiary.*
- *Property held in a trust.*
- *Retirement plans payable to named beneficiaries, including IRAs, Keogh accounts, and pensions.*
- *Totten trusts (a trust arrangement on a bank account payable to a named beneficiary at death) or pay-on-death bank accounts payable to a named beneficiary.*
- *Deeds in which the deceased held only a life estate, with the property going after death to a named beneficiary.*
- *Gifts made in contemplation of death.*

required for this waiver.) Payment options are treated differently for tax purposes and you'll want to ask your tax adviser how they'll affect your estate and tax planning.

IRAs (Individual Retirement Accounts) provide a ready means of cash when one spouse dies. If your spouse is named as the beneficiary, the proceeds will immediately become his or her property when you die. Like retirement benefits (and unlike assets distributed by a will or the state's intestate succession laws), they will pass without having to go through probate.

Life Insurance

Life insurance is often a good estate planning tool because you pay relatively little up front and your beneficiaries get much more when you die. When you name beneficiaries other than your estate, the money passes to them directly without going through probate. If most of your money is tied up in nonliquid assets like your company or real estate, life insurance gets cash into your beneficiaries' hands without their having to resort to a fire sale of other assets. Though procedures vary by company, usually the beneficiary informs the company in writing of the death, sends a copy of the death certificate, and receives a check, often within a few weeks.

In general, the older you are, the less your family needs large amounts of life insurance. To decide how much to purchase, begin by estimating the long- and short-term needs of your survivors. Next, estimate what will be covered by other sources such as savings, a pension, and other benefits. You'll want to buy enough life insurance to cover the difference.

Term insurance provides protection not for your entire life but only for a specified number of years; it's cheap when you're young but gets more expensive as you grow older. Nevertheless, it can be a good idea, especially if you're relatively young or are starting a business venture (banks sometimes insist that an entrepreneur's life be covered by such a policy as a condition of advancing capital).

Here are some examples of the long- and short-term needs your family may encounter. To really help minimize their worries, write up a plan with categories like these. Then, when the insurance proceeds are paid your survivors will know exactly how to budget the money they'll be receiving.

• **Costs of death.** Funeral, burial, and hospital bills . . . these are the most common expenses that result from death. Life insurance proceeds reach your survivors quickly and are useful for dealing with these expenses. Your family should expect to pay at least $5,000 to $10,000 to cover such costs, much more if medical costs were high and not covered by insurance. See chapter 11 for more information on such expenses.

• **Replacing lost income.** You don't want your family to have to sell property to support itself in the absence of your paycheck. Nor do you want your working spouse to have to take a second job. Experts say a family needs 75 percent of its former after-tax income to maintain its standard of living after the principal wage earner dies.

If you don't want your surviving spouse to have to work while raising the children, figure out how much it will take to support the family until the children are grown or at least able to care for themselves after school.

- **Grief fund.** Life insurance proceeds can support your family during the period of grief after your death so they don't have to go back to work too soon. This fund could equal up to several months of their normal income.

- **Educational expenses.** You can use life insurance proceeds (especially if paid into a trust) to set up a college fund for your children.

- **Mortgage-canceling life insurance.** Such a plan will pay off your mortgage when you die, so your survivors don't have to sell the family house. Or you can increase your life insurance by an amount sufficient to pay off the mortgage.

- **Emergency fund.** After figuring out the other needs, you might tack on several thousand dollars to help the family cope with unexpected emergencies.

Three Ways to Pay

If you own life insurance on your own life, you can have the proceeds distributed in three ways.

1. To beneficiaries. The company pays the proceeds directly to one or more beneficiaries named in your policy (or in a few states to their descendants). This is the quickest way to get the money to your survivors, and the proceeds pass free of income tax, except on the interest portion, and usually can't be touched by creditors. However, they may be subject to estate taxes if the proceeds, when added to the other assets in the estate, total more than $1 million (see chapter 8).

2. To your probate estate. If you choose this route, the proceeds will be distributed along with your other assets according to the terms of your will. (If you die without a will, your state's intestate succession laws will determine to whom the proceeds go.) However, they will be tied up in the probate process, will add to the cost of probate by making the estate larger, and will be subject to creditors' claims. You should do this only if your estate won't otherwise have enough money to pay debts and taxes. (See chapters 3 and 11.)

3. To a trust. If you make the proceeds payable to a trust—either one set up in your will or during your lifetime—they will be distributed like the other trust assets.

Paying the proceeds to a **life insurance trust** has several advantages:

- In many jurisdictions, creditors can't get at them.

- You will not have to pay estate tax on the proceeds if the policy was owned by the trust more than three years before your death and the trust is properly set up.

- If the trust is for the benefit of your minor children, you can avoid the expense and court involvement of having a guardian manage this property. By having the proceeds paid to a trust, the trustee will have control over it.

Who should own the policy? If it's in your name, the proceeds payable on death (not the value of the premiums paid) will be included in your estate for tax purposes. That might force you to pay estate taxes if it increases your estate beyond the current $1 million limit. If the beneficiary is your spouse, the **marital deduction** (see chapter 8) will enable your estate to escape taxes on the value of the policy. If someone else owns it (commonly, a life insurance trust), the proceeds aren't included in your estate, enabling you to reduce its taxable value. In any case, the recipient won't have to pay income taxes on the proceeds.

Life Estates

Life estates are different from gifts. Many older people choose to assign the family home to the children who have expressed an interest in living there after the parents have died. The parents retain what's called a **life estate interest** in the house, meaning they have the right to live there until they die and the property remains in their estate and is still taxable.

You can also choose to leave your children a life estate in family property that you want maintained down through the generations, like a home or china or other heirlooms. The children can live in the house or rent it to tenants during their lifetimes but must maintain it in good condition for the ultimate beneficiaries, usually the grandchildren.

If this sounds like a move appropriate for your family, talk to your lawyer about such an assignment. Conveying property through a life estate gives up control of your property, and a life estate is subject to complex legal rules and often causes more complications than it's worth.

Community Property

The laws of Puerto Rico and nine states—Arizona, California, Idaho, Louisiana, Nevada, New Mexico, Texas, Washington, and Wisconsin—provide that most property acquired during the marriage by either spouse is held equally by husband and wife as **community property**. (The major exceptions are property acquired by inheritance or gift.) When one spouse dies, his or her half of the community property passes either by will or intestacy; the other half belongs to the surviving spouse.

Unlike joint tenancy, community property isn't automatically transferred to the surviving spouse. When your spouse dies, you own only your share of the community property and your spouse must give his or her share to you (or anyone else) in a will. Often the dead spouse's share must be probated, but it depends on what state you live in. California, for example, no longer requires probate for property passing directly from one spouse to the other.

This arrangement can affect your estate planning in many ways. What if your spouse assumes his or her life insurance will give you enough money and leaves everything to your grown children? In a community property state, that means half of the community property goes to the children. They now own half the house, half the car, half the vacation place on the lake. If there wasn't much cash in the estate or in insurance paid to them, the only way they can really benefit from the will is to sell the property so they can share the proceeds. You'll either have to move out and get another car or they'll have to struggle along until you die. Married people in community property states should think long and hard before leaving property to anyone other than their spouse.

Community property laws affect how much of your family's property you can legally dispose of. When you're planning your estate, first determine what is community property and what is separate property. This is not always easy and the rules vary from state to state. Your lawyer can help you figure out which is which, so that you know what property you can transfer through estate planning.

Joint Tenancy:
Property You Own with Someone Else

Joint tenancy is a legal term that means, effectually, "co-ownership." If you and your spouse (like Darren and Samantha) buy a house or car in both your names as joint tenants, each of you is a co-owner. When one of you dies, the other joint tenant immediately owns it all regardless of what either of you says in your will.

Joint tenancy (sometimes called **survivorship**) can be a useful way to transfer property at death. Family automobiles and bank accounts often pass this way. Particularly in old age, people often place bank accounts or stocks in joint tenancy with their spouses, with one or more children, or with friends. When one of the co-owners dies, joint ownership in many states gives the other one instant access to the account to help pay bills. The transfer avoids probate. Many states have adopted the Uniform Probate Code, which creates a presumption that joint property is owned by the surviving owner at death.

Should you put property in joint tenancy as part of your estate planning? The answer will vary depending on your circumstances, but most estate planners urge caution, particularly if your estate is above the federal estate tax level. Even for small estates where taxes aren't an issue, however, there can be pitfalls. This is especially true of joint tenancy between a parent and one of several children, which can lead to litigation after the death of the parent.

ELEVEN TIMES WHEN JOINT TENANCY IS *NOT* A GOOD IDEA

Joint tenancy is not a panacea. Here are some tips about when to avoid it.

1. When you don't want to lose control. By giving someone co-ownership, you give him or her co-control. If you made your son co-owner of the house, you couldn't sell or mortgage it unless he agrees. (If he later marries, his wife may also have to agree.) If you do sell it, he may be entitled to part of the proceeds. Joint ownership of stock also means you've lost control. If you put your daughter on your stock accounts as a joint tenant, she could veto transactions.

2. When the co-owner's creditors might come after the money. If creditors come after your co-owner, they may be able to get part of the house or bank account. For example, creditors could attach your co-owner's half of your joint bank account, or get a **lien** (a claim upon property to satisfy a debt) on his or her half of the house, which could prevent you and the co-owner from selling it. (Of course, the creditors couldn't sell it either, but they'd have a club over the co-owner's—and your—head.)

3. When you can't be sure of your co-owner. You and your co-owner could have a falling out and the co-owner could take all the money out of the bank account. There's nothing you could do about it, since that person is a co-owner. What was created for convenience may turn into a nightmare. (Some states have **convenience accounts** that avoid some of these problems while allowing the co-owner to write checks and so on.) And, in many states, someone who jointly owns real estate can force a sale of the property without the owner's consent, no matter how small a portion he or she owns.

4. When you're using co-ownership to substitute for a will. Joint tenancy doesn't help if all the joint tenants die at once, so each tenant needs a will. Nor does it answer where your property goes if the younger joint tenant dies first. If you put one child's name on an account assuming he'll divide the money equally among the other children, know that he is on his honor and legally can do with it as he pleases. On top of all this, the transfer of property setting up this type of ownership could result in adverse income tax consequences when the surviving beneficiary sells the appreciated property.

5. When it might cause confusion after your death. Your mother makes you a joint owner of her bank account, so you can help her with her shopping and bill paying. Whom does she intend to own that account when she dies? Often, nasty lawsuits ensue between the original owner's estate and the surviving joint tenant. A common question: Did the owner put the property in joint tenancy to make a gift to the surviving tenant or was the joint tenant really a co-manager of the business or property or an agent of the owner?

6. When it won't speed the transfer of assets. Some states automatically freeze jointly owned accounts upon the death of one of the owners until the tax collector can examine it, so the surviving partner can't count on getting to the money immediately.

7. When it compromises tax planning. Careful planning to minimize the taxes on an estate can be thwarted by an inadvertently created joint tenancy which passes property outright to a beneficiary. For example, passing property by joint tenancy can increase estate taxes by preventing transfer to the children through a tax-avoiding **bypass trust** (see chapter 8). It can also increase gift taxes—the IRS may consider adding a joint tenant to be taxable gift giving. (There are, however, no gift tax implications for joint bank accounts until the co-owner makes a withdrawal, nor for savings bonds or stocks held by a broker.)

Many estate tax problems occur with **institutional revocable trusts** and **pay-on-death** forms of ownership of bank, broker, and mutual fund accounts and savings bonds. If you own any of these kinds of property, be sure you understand what happens to them when you die and plan accordingly.

Or suppose your aging mother asks if she can list you as a joint owner of her bank account; that way, you can buy her groceries, pay her bills, and so on. It would make things so much more convenient for her, since her memory isn't what it used to be and it's hard for her to get around. You agree.

Then, the unexpected happens: You're killed in a car accident. In many jurisdictions, the law will include the value of that bank account in your estate. (The money will revert to your mother, but for tax purposes the account could be considered part of your estate, along with everything else you owned that will pass to someone else upon your death.) If the account is large, your estate could suddenly grow from a modest one that had no tax concerns to one that will be hit hard by estate tax. Had your mother put that money in a trust or sheltered it in some other way, the tax could have been avoided. Now a good part of your children's inheritance will have to go instead to the federal government, and maybe your state government, too.

8. When you're in a shaky marriage. Your individual property becomes joint marital property once it's transferred into joint names.

9. When one of the co-owners becomes incompetent. If one of the co-owners becomes legally incompetent to make decisions, the court will appoint a **guardian** for him or her. This will put part of the property into a **guardianship**—making it cumbersome at best if the other joint tenant wants to sell a house or some stock.

10. When you don't want to transfer assets all at once. Joint tenancies deprive you of the flexibility of a will or trust, in which you can use gifts and shift assets to minimize taxes and pay out money over time to beneficiaries instead of giving it to them all at once.

11. When it raises taxes. In a community property state, you get a tax advantage from holding the assets as community property rather than in joint tenancy. (For tax purposes, both halves are valued at their worth upon transfer.) Thus, joint tenancy holdings could end up raising your tax bill.

Joint tenancy does have its advantages. It's inexpensive to create, for instance—you probably don't need a lawyer to buy an asset jointly. But the ultimate costs can far exceed these initial savings.

Most of the advantages of joint tenancy can be achieved using a simple **revocable living trust** (see chapter 5). And a device called a **beneficiary deed** can accomplish many benefits of joint tenancy with few of the risks. (Check with your attorney to see if it's available in your state and of use to you.) Also, your state may allow pay-on-death bank accounts that will give whomever you name as beneficiary access to the account at your death. This is a form of co-ownership that only becomes active when the account holder dies. It's a good way to get money to beneficiaries at death, but not before. Coupled with a power of attorney, it can retain ownership in your hands while you're alive while giving your beneficiary management authority. As noted above, though, it could have estate tax consequences, so check with your bank, accountant, or lawyer. Finally, chapter 8 discusses the possible tax advantages for spouses who put property in their names separately instead of owning it jointly.

Tenancy in Common

Don't confuse joint tenancies with **tenancies in common**. It's easy to do, especially when a state law deems an asset held in joint tenancy as titled "jointly as tenants in common." In joint tenancy, you and your spouse both own the *whole* house, which among other things means you must both agree to sell it. In tenancy in common, on the other hand, you each own a *half share* of the house and either of you may sell your half share without the other's consent (though not many buyers are interested in purchasing half a house). In tenancy in common, different partners can own unequal shares of the property. For example, your will might leave your vacation home to your three children as tenants in common but give the child who uses it most often or could manage it best a 51 percent share while the others divide the rest. (A better way would be to leave it in a trust for their benefit.)

Another difference: If you own an asset in joint tenancy with anyone and you die, ownership of that asset passes to the other joint tenant automatically. In a tenancy in common, your share passes as provided in your will or trust, with possible probate, estate tax, and other consequences. Tenancy in common can be less risky than joint tenancy and is especially useful for larger estates in which you give shares of property to the children during your lifetime. Ask your lawyer if it might help in your estate planning.

Inter Vivos Gifts: Giving It Away Before You Die

Federal tax laws now encourage people to transfer property through means other than their wills—often before they die. Trusts are the most common means, but you can also make cash gifts.

Are gifts made while you're alive (**inter vivos gifts**) a good idea? Maybe, especially if you have a large estate: They can help you avoid high death taxes. In some states, they might help you make an estate smaller and thus avoid full-fledged probate. Another advantage of giving property away before you die is that you get to see the recipient enjoy your generosity.

You have to watch out for a few things, however. Inter vivos gifts beyond a certain size are subject to gift taxes. Current law permits each person to make an unlimited number of tax-free gifts per year, as long as gifts are not more than $10,000 each ($20,000 if a couple makes the gift). Recipients don't have to be related to you. You can also make gifts to trusts and to charities.

You should state in your will that any gifts you have made before you died to a beneficiary of your will or trust will not be considered an **advancement** (a gift that is to be subtracted from the amount a beneficiary is left in a will or trust). If you don't, the probate court in some states may subtract the amount of the gift from the amount you gave him or her in the will. For example, suppose you write a will that leaves your son $25,000. A month later you give him $10,000 for a year of college. Then, a month after that, you die. If your will didn't state that any gifts, like the $10,000, weren't advancements, the probate court might subtract the $10,000 from the $25,000, and your son will wind up with $10,000 less than you intended. If you do intend that the gift be an advancement, it's a good idea to put that in writing, so the court will reduce the amount he'll receive through your will or your state's intestate succession laws.

The Bottom Line

This chapter doesn't cover all the ways of transferring property without a will. Other strategies, such as taking against the will and prenuptial agreements, are covered in chapter 7. The main thing is to be aware of the kinds of property that a will doesn't cover, so you can use them in your estate planning if they're right for you. You should also keep records of all these items and your other assets in a single place and, to avoid confusion, mention the records in your will. This precaution makes estate planning easier for you and locating your assets easier for your family after you die.

CHAPTER THREE

■

Making a Will

A WILL IS a person's revocable document that provides for transfer of property at death, usually designating someone as executor to carry it out. Wills have been with us since the first days of recorded history. Archaeologists have found 4,500-year-old hieroglyphics in Egyptian tombs that state the authors' wishes to leave property to others. Bible readers recall that Jacob left Joseph a larger inheritance than his brothers received and the trouble that that caused.

Whether in ancient Egypt or modern America, all wills are different. What you put in yours depends on what property you have, to whom you want it to go, the dynamics of your family, and so on. This chapter sets out some of the factors you may want to consider in making your will. (For what to do if you later decide to change or revoke it, see chapter 9.)

THE SEVEN ESSENTIALS OF A VALID WILL

To be valid, your will doesn't have to conform to a specific formula. For example, in states that recognize handwritten, unwitnessed wills, some wills scrawled on the back of envelopes have stood up in court. However, there are certain elements that usually must be present.

1. You must be of **legal age to make a will**. This is eighteen in most states, but may be several years older or younger in some places—check with a lawyer if you need to know.

29

2. You must be of **sound mind and memory**, which means that you should know you're **executing** (formally completing and signing) a will, know the general nature and extent of your property, and know the objects of your bounty, that is, your spouse, descendants, and other relatives who would ordinarily be expected to share in your estate. Although you do not have to be found mentally incompetent by a court for your will to be challenged on those grounds, the law presumes that a **testator** (person making a will) was of sound mind and memory and the standard for proving otherwise is very high—much more than mere absentmindedness or forgetfulness.

Disgruntled relatives who want to challenge a will occasionally use this "sound mind and memory" requirement to attack the testator's mental capacity. So if you suspect that someone might try this, take care to have evidence to rebut evidence that might be submitted in a suit to invalidate the will. The execution of a will is sometimes videotaped and kept on file, so if someone raises a question after the testator dies, the videotape can be good evidence of **testamentary capacity**—that is, competence to make a will.

3. The will must have a substantive provision that disposes of your property and it must indicate your intent to make the document your final word on what happens to your property— that is, you really intended it to *be* a will.

4. The will must be voluntarily signed by the testator unless illness or accident or illiteracy prevents it, in which case you can direct that your lawyer or one of the witnesses sign for you. But having someone sign for you requires a lawyer's guidance or at least knowledge of your state's law, since an invalid signature could void the will.

5. Although **oral wills** are permitted in limited circumstances in some states if they meet legal requirements, wills must usually be written and witnessed. The will scrawled on an envelope won't work in these states. To be safe, don't handwrite a will if you can avoid it.

KINDS OF WILLS

Here's a brief glossary of terms used in the law for various kinds of wills:

- **Simple will.** Provides for the outright distribution of assets for an uncomplicated estate.

- **Testamentary trust will.** Sets up one or more trusts for some of your assets to go to after you die.

- **Pourover will.** Leaves some of your assets in a trust that you had already established before you signed the will.

- **Holographic will.** Unwitnessed and in the testator's handwriting, such wills are recognized in about twenty states.

- **Oral will** (also called **nuncupative will**). Spoken, not written down; a few states permit this type of will.

- **Joint will.** One document, which might constitute a contract, that covers both a husband and wife (or any two people). Joint wills often result in litigation.

- **Living will.** Not really a will at all, since it has force while you are still alive and doesn't dispose of property, but often executed at the same time you make your will. Tells doctors and hospitals whether you wish life support in the event you are terminally ill or, as a result of accident or illness, cannot be restored to consciousness. See chapter 12.

6. Though some states do allow informal oral and written wills in certain circumstances, all states have standards for formal wills. Writing a **formal will** and following these standards helps assure that your wishes will be followed after your death. In almost all states, the signing of a formal will must be witnessed by at least two adults who understand what they are witnessing and are competent to testify in court. There have to be three witnesses in Vermont and New Hampshire, three *plus a notary* in Puerto Rico. In most states, the witnesses have to be **disinterested** (i.e., not getting anything under your will). If they aren't, you run the risk of voiding certain provisions in the will, opening it to challenge or invalidating it entirely.

7. A formal will must be properly **executed**, which means that it contains a statement at the end attesting that it is your will, the date and place of signing, and the fact that you signed it in the presence of the witnesses who then also signed it in your presence and watched each other sign. Most states allow so-called **self-proving affidavits**, which eliminate the necessity of having the witnesses testify in court that they witnessed the signing; the affidavit is proof enough. In other states, if the witnesses have since died or are unavailable, the court may have to get someone else to verify the legitimacy of their signatures.

If your will doesn't meet these conditions, it might be disallowed by a court and your estate would then be distributed according to any previous will or under your state's intestacy laws.

WHO CAN WRITE A WILL

Legally, you don't have to use a lawyer to write your will. If it meets the legal requirements in your state, a will is valid whether you wrote it with a lawyer's help or not.

Nonetheless, studies show that more than 85 percent of Americans who have wills used a lawyer's help in preparing them.

Below are your alternatives and considerations to take into account in deciding which to use.

Doing It Yourself

Several alternatives are absolutely free but not often used. For example, **oral wills** are permissible in less than half the states, sometimes under very limited circumstances, such as when they are uttered in a final illness. Also, oral wills often apply only to personal property. They raise immense problems of proof.

Handwritten, unwitnessed wills are valid in less than half the states and effective in disposing of more kinds of property. Nonetheless, they're not recommended. Since they rarely follow legal formalities, it's sometimes hard to prove that they are intended to be wills—or intended to be your *last* will—and they are vulnerable to fraud and often don't cover all the testator's assets.

Soldiers' and seamen's wills are permitted by about half the

LIVING TRUSTS AND WILLS

*Some people think that in order to avoid probate, they should avoid a will and instead use a living trust to transfer property between generations. A living trust can be a very useful part of estate planning (see chapter 5 for details). However, it alone can't accomplish many of the most important goals of estate planning. For example, you may have to have a will to name a personal guardian for your children even if you have a trust. And even with a living trust, you'll need a simple will to dispose of property that you didn't put into the trust. In addition, many trusts are funded at death by property given to them by a **pourover will**. Probate is also no longer as bad as it once was. So preparing at least a simple, auxiliary will is recommended for just about everyone.*

states. They allow people actually serving in the armed forces to dispose of their wages and personal property orally or in an informal written document. Often, they're valid only during wartime when the will maker is in a hostile zone, and they usually cease to be valid after a certain time that varies by state.

Statutory wills are another free alternative available in a few states. A statutory will is a form that has been created by state law. Since the statutory will includes all the formalities, all you have to do is get a copy at a stationery store, fill it out, and have it witnessed, and you have a valid will. Unfortunately, these wills are very limited. They assume you want to leave everything to your spouse and children and provide for few other gifts. And you must follow the form—they can't legally be changed, though they can be modified by codicils that add specific bequests, etc.

In recent years, a number of books and computerized will kits have come on the market that claim to enable you to make your own will. The cost of a book may run $20 or more, the cost of a kit $70 or more. For simple estates—involving little money and other assets, and in which everything is to go to few people—they might be a viable alternative. However, make sure that a given book or kit is up-to-date and thorough, especially since probate laws vary from state to state. The computerized kits are easier than the books to fit into your estate plan—typically, they guide you through a will with computer prompts that let you alter it according to your needs.

Doing it this way may not be easy, however. Do-it-yourself books and kits, some lawyers say, have caused more work for lawyers (and bills for clients) than they have avoided. There's a famous case about one man who thought he'd get two wills for the price of one will kit. He made a form will for himself, then took that and substituted his wife's name for his own in the signature clause and the introductory clause. But he failed to change the name of the beneficiaries—meaning that when his wife died, she left all her property to herself! This one, of course, ended up in court, at a substantial cost to the surviving husband.

Once you begin totaling up all your assets, you may be surprised to find that your estate is larger than you thought. At the same time, family relationships are becoming more complicated. Today, a do-it-yourself will might not do the job and may prove costly in the long run.

Using a Lawyer

The cost of having a will drawn up professionally depends on the size and complexity of your estate, the going rates for lawyers in your area, your lawyer's experience, and so on.

About 74 million Americans belong to **group legal service plans**. These plans enable members to get legal services either free or at reduced cost. In many programs, simple wills are either free or cost far less than the going rate. (More complex work such as seeing a will through probate may not be covered.) More comprehensive estate planning and preparation of other documents are available from lawyers at a reduced hourly rate. About 90 percent of plans are available to members of certain organizations (like AARP, the military, or a union), or to workers in certain industries as a result of collective bargaining agreements. Some of these plans have no fee at all to the participant; others may have a modest fee. About 10 percent of plans are available to individuals, including one through the Signature Group of Montgomery Ward.

WHICH LAW APPLIES?

*The laws of the state of your **domicile**, that is, where your primary home is located, determine generally what happens to your personal property. Distribution of your real property (real estate) is governed by the laws of the state in which the property is located. If you do own homes or property in different states, it's a good idea to make sure that the provisions comply with the laws of the appropriate state. You can't rely on a will drafted by a lawyer for your brother in Oregon if your primary home is located in, say, Louisiana (especially in Louisiana, which follows the Napoleonic Code and is legally unique in the United States).*

Legal clinics are another low-cost alternative. They can prepare your will for modest amounts because legal assistants do much of the work under a lawyer's guidance. That work often consists of adapting standard computerized forms to fit the needs of the client. If you have a small, simple estate, the cost may be modest and you have the benefit of professional advice and reassurance that your will meets the standards for validity in your state.

If you use a private lawyer, you may find that the first consultation is free. Ask one to give you a price or range of prices for preparing a will or estate plan; it might be cheaper than you think. Before you give the final go-ahead to draw up your will, ask the estimated cost (or at least a range of likely costs).

You should use a lawyer if you own a business, if your estate is substantial (a $1 million estate makes tax planning a factor under current law), or if you anticipate a challenge to the will from a disgruntled relative or anyone else.

As noted in chapter 1, a skillfully drawn will generally saves you money in the long run. By giving the executor (the person you choose to administer your estate after you die) authority to act efficiently, by saying that a **surety bond** (which protects your estate if your executor does not perform his or her duties) will not be required, and by directing that the involvement of the probate court be kept to a minimum, you can save your family money.

WHY A JOINT WILL IS A BAD IDEA

*Both spouses should execute separate wills. A **joint will** is a contract between two people that requires the consent of both to modify. It generally provides that each spouse's property will go to the other, and then spells out what will happen to the property when the second person dies. Because both parties have to agree to modify such wills, they often aren't revised as frequently as they should be, whether because of family disagreements or just a double dose of inertia. A joint will can keep the survivor from using the property as he or she wishes, doesn't allow for circumstances that change after the will was made, and may be impossible to revoke. It frequently results in litigation if, after one of the makers dies, the survivor makes a new will.*

WRITING A WILL

Freedom of Disposition

After your lawyer has a good idea of what you want and what your assets are, he or she will probably suggest various options to help you achieve your objectives. In general, you can pick who you want your property to go to and leave it in whatever proportions you want.

There are exceptions, however. For example, a surviving husband or wife may be entitled to a **statutory share** of the estate regardless of the will. This is a percentage set by state law. (You or your spouse can voluntarily give up this legal protection in a pre- or postnuptial agreement.) Otherwise, you can disinherit anyone, but if you're disinheriting a family member, you should do so specifically, not by omission, and provide for distribution to others (see chapters 6 and 7 for details). In some states, such as Florida, a surviving spouse is entitled by law to the family home as a **homestead right**. Though your spouse can try to give it to someone else in the will, you have to approve or the property is yours. Some states limit how much you can leave to a charity if you have a surviving spouse or children or if you died soon after making the provision (under the assumption someone exerted undue influence on you).

Most states impose some restrictions on conditions listed in wills that are bizarre, illegal, or against public policy of the state. For example, if you wanted to set up an institute to promote terrorism and violent overthrow of the government, the probate court would probably throw out the bequest.

Some people try to make their influence felt beyond the grave by attaching conditions to a gift made in the will (as opposed to the purely advisory language in a letter of intent). Most lawyers advise against this; courts don't like such conditions, and you're inviting a will contest if you try to tie them to a gift. You can't require your daughter to divorce her no-account husband to claim her inheritance from you; nor can your husband make your inheritance contingent on a promise you'll never remarry; nor can you force that secular humanist son-in-law to go to church every Sunday. For the most part, though, it's your call.

CLAUSE BY CLAUSE

There's no set formula for what goes into a will. There are some things you might want to think about if you fall into certain categories—younger couples, older couples, single people, divorced people, and so on. Chapters 6 and 7 discuss some of the needs and options different people might have in planning their estates.

Below are the more common clauses of a basic will, following the order of clauses of the sample will in this chapter, to illustrate some typical will contents.

Funeral Expenses and Payment of Debts

Your debts don't die with you; your estate is still liable for them, and your executor needs no authority to pay them off.

If your debts exceed your assets, your state law will prescribe the order in which the debts must be paid by category. Funeral expenses and expenses of administering the will usually get first priority. Family allowances, taxes, and last illness expenses will also appear near the top of the list. If you want certain creditors to be paid off first, ask your lawyer how to ensure this will happen under your state's particular law.

As for funeral directions, while you can put them in your will, be aware that they might not be found until after you're buried. It's best to put these in a separate document (see chapter 11).

You can also forgive any debts someone owes you by saying so in your will.

Gifts of Personal Property

It's important to carefully identify all recipients of your largesse, including their addresses and relationship to you. There are too many cases of people leaving property to "my cousin John," not realizing that more than one person might fit that description. Or you leave something to "my sister's husband" and she later divorces him and remarries—who gets the gift? A court might have to decide.

If you have several children or other relatives in the same category (cousins, siblings, etc.) and you want them to divide your estate or some portion of it equally, you should state that you are giving the gift to them as a class ("my cousins and not their descendants") and not as individuals ("Mutt and Jeff"). That way, if one of them dies, the others would take the whole gift. Otherwise, the dead cousin's share would **lapse** (be cancelled) and might be distributed by intestacy. On the other hand, if you definitely do want a beneficiary's children to take a gift if he or she predeceases you, you would use language that indicates this; typically, "to my cousins, A, B, and C, but if any of them does not survive me, his share to his descendants, **per stirpes**" (Latin, meaning that these descendants split the share that would have gone to the dead cousin). This is technical territory that shouldn't be entered without the advice of an attorney, but the main thing to remember about gifts to a class is this: If you have several beneficiaries, use language that will account for the possibility of one of the class dying before you do.

For similar reasons, you should usually be specific about the gifts you are making. Don't just leave "household property" to someone, because that category is vague enough to spark a dispute in court (or at least in the family). Spell out the items ("stereo equipment, clothing, books, cash") or just omit any mention at all and let them pass through the residuary clause (discussed below).

On the other hand, in cases where the specific item of property might change between the time you write the will and the time you die, you might want to be more general in your phrasing—leaving your son not "my 1986 Yugo" but "the car I own when I die" instead. The same approach applies to stocks or bank accounts; the bank might be taken over by another bank or the stock sold. Better to include a general description or leave a dollar amount or fractional share of your estate.

Make sure the language you use in giving the gift is unambiguous: "I give ...," "I direct that ...," and so on. Wishy-washy terms like "It is my wish that ..." might be taken to be merely an expression of hope, not an order. At the very least, such **precatory language** could invite a court challenge.

In general, it's simpler for your executor if you leave your tangible personal property to people in broad but specific categories ("all my furniture") rather than passing it on piece by piece ("my kitchen table") to many different people. If you want specific gifts of sentimental value to go to certain people, consider giving them to those people before you die, so you can witness their pleasure (and, if your estate is large, lower estate taxes). Some attorneys advise leaving most items to one or two people and then writing a **letter of intent** that advises those people about how you want them to spend that money or distribute those items. Some states have laws providing for these letters but some do not. That means *letters of intent may not be legally binding.* Use them only with people you can trust. (One way to handle specific bequests of personal property is through a **tangible personal property memorandum**, or TPPM. See chapter 9 for details.)

Remember also that personal property can include intangible assets like insurance policies. If you own a policy on your spouse's life, that policy and the cash value of the premiums paid into it can be passed on through your will. Bank accounts, certain employee benefits, and stock options are also intangible assets. These should not pass in a TPPM, but in the will itself, perhaps in the residuary clause (see pages 41–42).

Avoid leaving shares of stock of a designated publicly held company to a single beneficiary. It may increase substantially in value and upset your plan with respect to other beneficiaries. Or it may go down in value. It would be better to give that person a specified percentage or fraction of your estate.

Finally, if you want several people to share a gift, be careful to specify what percentage of ownership each will have. If you don't, the court will probably presume that you intended the beneficiaries to share equally. Most lawyers counsel against shared gifts because it means several people have to agree on use of the property and one co-owner may be able to force a sale. But there are some indivisible assets—a house, typically—where you may have little choice but to let more than one person share in the gift. If so, talk to the beneficiaries first and make sure they agree on how they'll jointly use and manage the gift. And be sure to designate alternative beneficiaries (usually the others who will share in the gift) in case one of them dies before you do.

This section of your will can also be used to give gifts to institutions and charities as well as to people. You can save on taxes by giving charitable gifts wisely.

Gifts of Real Estate

Most people prefer that their spouses receive the family home. If the home isn't held in **joint tenancy** (**survivorship**), you should have instructions about what will happen to it in your will.

It is possible to give what lawyers call a **life estate**. This is giving something to a person, to use for as long as he or she lives.

After he or she dies, it reverts to your estate or passes to someone else (see chapter 2 for more on this). It's a way of assuring, for example, that your husband will have the use of your house while he lives, but that it will pass to the children of your first marriage after he dies. Specify what, if any, expenses he is to pay while occupying the property: cost of maintenance, mortgage payment, repairs, taxes, insurance, heat and air-conditioning, etc. The rules governing such transfers, or any transfers different from a **fee simple** outright transfer of ownership, are so complicated that you must use a lawyer to make such a gift properly.

If you die before you've paid off the mortgage on your house, your estate might have to pay it off. If you're afraid this will drain the estate too much, or if you want the recipient of the house to continue to pay the mortgage, you must specify that in your will. If you haven't paid off the family house and you're afraid your survivors can't afford to, you may be able to buy mortgage-canceling insurance to pay it off.

Residuary Clause

This is one of the most crucial parts of a will, covering all assets not specifically disposed of by the will. You will probably accumulate assets after you write your will, and if you haven't specifically given an asset to someone, it won't pass through the will—unless you have a **residuary clause** that, as Lyndon Johnson used to say of grandmother's nightdress, covers everything. If your will omits a residuary clause, the assets not left specifically to anyone would pass on through the intestate succession laws, possibly after long delays and extensive court involvement.

Any of your property that's not controlled by other parts of your will is said to fall into your **residuary estate**. All property in this imaginary category is controlled by the residuary clause. No matter how small your residuary estate seems at the time you write your will, you should be sure your will distributes it. If you leave it to more than one person, specify the percentages or fractions if other than equal.

The residuary clause distributes assets that you might not have anticipated owning, such as property you inherit after writing your will. And normally anything you own in joint tenancy would pass automatically to the other tenant at your death and so you wouldn't include it in your will. But what if the joint tenant dies before you? Your estate would then probably own the entire asset, and your residuary clause would ensure that it goes to someone you care about.

Testamentary Trusts

As we'll see in the next chapter, you can set up a **testamentary trust** in your will or have your will distribute funds from your estate into a trust you had previously established (your will would then be a **pourover will**). You would normally do so in a separate clause in your will.

What If?

You should always play the "what if?" game and try to figure out where a gift would go if something unexpected happened—then account for that possibility in your will. What if one of your beneficiaries dies before you do? In that event, the gift you made to the dead person is said to **lapse** and the gift goes back into your residuary estate, to be distributed to whomever you made the residuary beneficiary. Most states, however, have **anti-**

THE GREATEST WILL OF ALL

Shakespeare, a Will himself, also recognized the dramatic power of wills. In Julius Caesar, *Antony delivers a funeral oration to "friends, Romans, countrymen" after the dictator's assassination. While claiming that he came not to praise Caesar, by reciting the clause in Caesar's will that left every Roman 75 drachmas and his "arbours and . . . orchards" as parkland, the wily Antony managed to turn the public against the democratic assassins and inherit Caesar's political power.*

In the climactic scene in The Merchant of Venice, *Portia's father's will instructs potential suitors for her that they must choose correctly among gold, silver, and lead caskets in order to win her hand.*

lapse statutes providing that if a beneficiary who is your child or descendant predeceases you, that beneficiary's descendants would receive the gift. So if you left your shoe collection to your daughter Imelda and she died before you did, in a state with an anti-lapse statute the footwear would go to Imelda's descendants. In a state without an anti-lapse statute, it would go to whomever you had named to receive your residuary estate. You can also name a **contingent beneficiary** who will get a gift if the primary recipient should die first.

Executors

It helps to spell out certain powers the **executor** (or, as he or she is called under the laws of some states, the **personal representative**) can have in dealing with your estate: to buy, lease, sell, and mortgage real estate; to borrow and lend money; to exercise various tax options. Giving the executor this kind of flexibility can save months of delay and many dollars by allowing him or her to cope with unanticipated situations. If you run a business, be sure to give your executor specific power to continue the business—or enter into new business arrangements. If you don't, the law may require that the business be liquidated or sold.

A General Tip

Be sure to carefully proofread your will, whether you write it yourself or your lawyer does. Does page 9 follow page 8? If you are leaving percentages of your estate to different people, do the percentages add up to 100?

SAMPLE BASIC WILL (ANNOTATED)

There is no standard, legally foolproof will. State laws vary, as do the needs of people making wills. This sample is designed only to give you an idea what a will might look like and why certain language is in it to prevent problems. Your own will should be crafted to fit your particular needs and wishes.

I, Tess Tatrix, residing at 1 Wilthereza Way, any town, any state, declare this to be my Will, and I revoke all prior wills and codicils.

The opening sentence should make it clear that this document is intended to be your will, give your name, place of residence, and revoke any previous wills and **codicils** (amendments to previous wills). This can help avoid a court battle if someone should produce an earlier will.

ARTICLE I:
Funeral Expenses and Payment of Debts

I authorize my executors to pay my enforceable unsecured debts and funeral expenses, the expenses of my last illness, and the expenses of administering my estate.

In most states, the executor is required by law to pay enforceable unsecured debts from the estate. In those states, this clause is unnecessary unless there may be a question whether they should be paid by the executor or the trustee of a revocable trust. This clause gives your executor authority to pay the funeral home, court costs, and hospital expenses. Using the term "enforceable" prevents creditors from reviving debts you are no longer obliged to pay, usually those discharged in bankruptcy. And the term "unsecured" prevents a court from interpreting this clause to mean that your estate must pay off your mortgage or other secured debts that you probably don't want immediately paid off. You would probably want your executor to keep payments current on your mortgage so that your estate does not risk losing the property. Nothing in this language prevents that, but you could make it explicit if you preferred.

ARTICLE II:
Money and Personal Property

I give all my tangible personal property, and all policies and proceeds of insurance covering such property, to my husband, Tex. If he does not survive me, I give that property to those of my children who survive me, in equal shares, to be divided among them by my executors in their absolute discretion after consultation with my children. My executors may pay out of my estate the expenses of delivering tangible personal property to beneficiaries.

This gives your personal property to your spouse. If there are particular items that you want to go to other people (such as heirlooms, jewelry, professional equipment, and so on), you should enumerate them and the persons you want them to go to in a separate clause (e.g., "I give my Beatles albums to my friend William Shears") and note that Article II excludes those items. Some people will use separate clauses for **legacies** (dispositions of money) and **bequests** (dispositions of tangible personal property). Note the important clause that accounts for the possibility that your spouse will die first. The clause on insurance means that if some property you owned was destroyed (perhaps in the event that caused your death, like a car wreck), your heirs will receive the insurance proceeds, not the mangled car.

ARTICLE III: Real Estate

I give all my residences, subject to any mortgages or encumbrances thereon, and all policies and proceeds of insurance covering such property, to my husband, Tex. If he does not survive me, I give that property to _____ .

Most people want their spouse to keep the family home. In some states, particularly community property states, it's sometimes preferable to leave your residence to your spouse in a marital trust. Also, note that this language requires your spouse, not your estate, to pay off the remaining balance of the mortgage through regular monthly payments or on an accelerated schedule if your spouse prefers.

ARTICLE IV: Residuary Clause

I give the rest of my estate (called my residuary estate) to my husband, Tex. If he does not survive me, I give my residuary

estate to those of my children who survive me, in equal shares among them and the descendants of a deceased child of mine, to take their ancestor's share per stirpes.

Usually the residuary clause begins "I give all the rest, residue, and remainder of my estate . . ." because lawyers are afraid to change tried-and-true formulas and for decades legal documents never used one word when a half-dozen would do. However, this plain-English form will also work. This clause covers any property you own or are entitled to that somehow wasn't covered by the preceding clauses.

ARTICLE V: Taxes

I direct my executors to pay all estate, inheritance, and succession taxes (including any interest and penalties thereon) payable by reason of my death.

As we'll see in chapter 8, death often is followed by taxes. Your will should strive to ensure that the people who benefit from your gifts also pay any related taxes.

One common mistake by people who use a living trust as well

as a will is to make the beneficiary of the estate different from the people benefiting from the trust. The same problem comes up when there are significant specific gifts and the residuary beneficiaries are different from the recipients of the specific gifts. In such cases, those paying the taxes are not those who receive the most property, an arrangement that can unfairly saddle some beneficiaries with the whole tax bill and at worst even bankrupt the estate.

Often, a provision apportioning taxes to taxable transfers is used to make sure that each recipient of a taxable gift pays his or her fair share. Additional language is sometimes used to apportion tax credits.

ARTICLE VI: Minors

If under this will any property shall be payable outright to a person who is a minor, my executors may, without court approval, pay all or part of such property to a parent or guardian of that minor or to a custodian under the Uniform Transfers to Minors or Uniform Gifts to Minors Acts. No bond shall be required for any such payment.

This clause gives your executors discretion to make sure any gift to a minor will be given in a way that's appropriate to his or her age. (The Uniform Acts make it possible to easily set up accounts for the benefit of minors but administered by adults.) The "no bond" language is intended to save the estate money.

ARTICLE VII: Fiduciaries

I appoint my husband, Tex, as executor of this will. If he is unable or unwilling to act, or resigns, I appoint my daughter, Ellie

Mae, and my son, Jethro, as successor co-executors. If either co-executor is unable or unwilling to act, the survivor shall serve as executor. My executor shall have all the powers allowable to executors under the laws of this state. I direct that no bond or security of any kind shall be required of any executor.

If you set up a trust in the will, you could name the trustees in this clause as well. The "bond or security" clause is designed to save the estate money.

ARTICLE VIII: Simultaneous Death Clause

If my (husband/wife) and I die under such circumstances that the order of our deaths cannot be readily ascertained, my (husband/wife) shall be deemed to have predeceased me. No person, other than my spouse, shall be deemed to have survived me if such person dies within 30 days after my death. This article modifies all provisions of this will accordingly.

This clause helps avoid the sometimes time-consuming problems that occur if you and your spouse die together in an accident. Your spouse's will should contain an identical clause; even though it seems contradictory to have two wills each directing that the other spouse died first, since each will is probated by itself this allows the estate plan set up in each will to go forward as you planned.

The second sentence exists to prevent the awkward legal complications that can ensue if someone dies between the time you die and the time the estate is divided up. Instead of passing through two probate processes, your gift to a beneficiary who dies shortly after you do would go to whomever you would have wanted it to go had the intended beneficiary died before you did. Most such gifts go into the residuary estate.

ARTICLE IX: Guardian

If my husband does not survive me and I leave minor children surviving me, I appoint as guardian of the persons and property of my minor children my uncle Ernest Entwistle. He shall have custody of my minor children and shall serve without bond. If he does not qualify or for any reason ceases to serve as guardian, I appoint as successor guardian my cousin Kevin Moon.

I have signed this will this _____ day of _____, 19____.

_____
(legal signature)

SIGNED AND DECLARED by Tess Tatrix on _____ to be her will, in our presence, who at her request, in her presence and in the presence of each other, all being present at the same time, have signed our names as witnesses.

_____
(signature)

Blair Witness
Address

_____
(signature)

I. Witness
Address

Self-Proving Affidavit

STATE OF _____

COUNTY OF _____

Each of the undersigned, Blair Witness and I. Witness, both on oath, says that:

The attached will was signed by Tess Tatrix, the testator named in the will, on the _____ day of _____, 19____ at the law offices of Lex Juris, 5440 Orfite St., Geo, Washington.

When she signed the will, Tess Tatrix declared the instrument to be her last will.

Each of us then signed his or her name as a witness at the end of this will at the request of Tess Tatrix and in her presence and in the presence of each other.

Tess Tatrix was, at the time of executing this will, over the age of eighteen years and, in our opinions, of sound mind and memory and not under any restraint or in any respect incompetent to make a will.

The will was executed as a single original instrument.

Each of us was acquainted with Tess Tatrix when the will was executed and makes this affidavit at her request.

_____
(signature)

Blair Witness
Address

_____
(signature)

I. Witness
Address

Sworn to before me this _____ day of _____, 19____.

_____

(signature and official seal)

Notary Public

AFTER THE WILL IS WRITTEN

Executing the Will

After you've drawn up your will, there remains one step: the formal legal procedure called **executing the will**. This requires witnesses to your signing the will. In all states, the testimony of at least two witnesses is needed as proof of the will's validity. In some states, the witnesses must actually show up in court to attest to this, but in a growing number of states a will that is formally executed (with the signatures notarized in some states) and has a self-proving affidavit attached is considered to be **self-proved** and may be used without testimony of witnesses or other proof.

Whom should you pick to be your witnesses? The witnesses should have no potential conflict of interest—which means they should absolutely not be people who receive any gifts under the will or who might benefit from your death. You needn't bring them with you to your lawyer's office; typically, some employees of your lawyer will witness the signing. The witnesses will watch you sign the will and then sign a statement attesting to this.

Where to Keep Your Will

It's not a bad idea to make a few _unsigned_ copies of your will and have them available for ready reference, but to avoid confusion you should sign only one original. This—and only this— will be your legally valid will. Keep it in a safe place, such as your safe-deposit box or your lawyer's office. Some jurisdictions will permit you to lodge the will with the probate court for a nominal fee, but in some places, that makes the will a public record. If privacy is paramount for you, you should ask your lawyer or the probate office how best to accomplish this.

You should also keep a record of other estate-planning documents with your will, such as a trust agreement, IRAs, insurance polices, income savings plans such as 401(k) plans, government savings bonds (if payable to another person), and retirement plans.

What if you lose your will? Have your lawyer draw up a new one as soon as possible and execute it with all the necessary formalities. If your family situation, state of residence, or income haven't changed, your lawyer should be able to use copies of your lost will as a guide.

While many people keep their wills in their safe-deposit boxes at a bank, in some jurisdictions the law requires those boxes to be sealed immediately after death until the estate is sorted out. Needless to say, if your will, cemetery deeds, or burial instructions are inside that box—sorting things out might get pretty complicated. If you do keep it in a safe-deposit box, make sure to provide that someone else (and certainly the executor you name) can get at it when you die. Tell your executor and your beneficiaries where the will is located and make sure your executor (or someone you trust) has authority (and a key!) to open the box after your death. Many estates have gone through long probate delays because the bank didn't have permission to let anyone open the safe-deposit box except the person who had just died. If you name a bank as executor or co-executor, deliver the original will to the bank for safekeeping.

It's okay to store *copies* of the will in your home. Personal papers such as your birth certificate, citizenship records, marriage certificate, coin collections, jewelry, heirlooms, medals, and so on may be kept in your safe-deposit box. Such financial records as securities, mortgage documents, contracts, leases, and deeds are also safe to store.

What about a trust agreement? Unlike a will, a trust may have more than one original, in which case there will be language saying something like "This trust is executed in four counterparts, each of which has the force of an original." Your trustee, successor trustee, and lawyer should each have a copy. And every time you amend the trust, be sure to have the amendment in a separate copy so indicated and signed by you. Unless the amendment is a **complete restatement of the trust** (i.e., a complete reworking of the trust), attach an executed copy to each signed copy of the trust if possible.

CHAPTER FOUR

∎

Trusts

LIKE A WILL, a trust is a very useful instrument in the estate-planning arsenal. Estates can be as diverse as people, and the flexibility of a trust makes it useful for many different needs. A trust can do a number of things a will can't do as well unless the will establishes a trust or pours over into a trust.

• If you have a trust, your trustee can manage assets efficiently if you should die and your beneficiaries are minor children or others not up to the responsibility of handling the estate.

• A trust can protect your privacy; unlike a will, a trust is confidential, though a few states require that a trust be registered.

• Depending on how it is written, and on state law, a trust can protect your assets by reducing taxes.

• If it is a living trust, the trustee can manage property for you while you're alive, providing a way to care for you if you should become disabled. A living trust also avoids probate, lowers estate administration costs, and speeds transfer of your assets to beneficiaries after your death.

Should you have a trust? It depends on the size of your estate and the purpose of the trust. For example, if you mainly want a living trust to protect assets from taxes and probate but your estate is under the current federal tax floor and small enough to qualify for quick and inexpensive probate in your state, some lawyers would tell you it isn't worth the cost. If, however, you want to avoid a court hearing if you become incompetent or unable to provide for yourself, or you want to provide for grandchildren, minor children, or relatives with a disability that makes it difficult for them to manage money, a trust has many advantages.

This chapter discusses general principles of trusts and their common uses. To learn about amending or revoking a trust, see chapter 9. It should help you determine if one is suitable for you. The next chapter covers the most popular trust: the revocable living trust.

WHAT IS A TRUST?

A trust is a legal relationship in which a **trustee** (which can be one person or a qualified trust company) holds property for the benefit of another (the **beneficiary**). The property can be any kind of real or personal property—money, real estate, stocks, bonds, collections, business interests, personal possessions, and other tangible assets. It is often established by one person for the benefit of another. In those cases, it involves at least three people: the **grantor** (the person who creates the trust, also known as the **settlor** or **donor**), the trustee (who holds and manages the property), and one or more beneficiaries (who are entitled to the benefits).

It may be helpful to think of a trust as a contract between the grantor and the trustee. The grantor transfers property to the trustee for certain purposes. The trustee agrees to manage and distribute the property in the way specified.

Putting property in trust transfers it from your personal ownership to the trustee, who holds the property for your beneficiaries. The trustee has **legal title** to the trust property. For most purposes, the law looks at these assets as if they were now owned by the trustee. For example, trusts have separate taxpayer identification numbers (except in a revocable trust when the grantor and trustee are the same person; then, the grantor's Social Security number can be used). But trustees are not the full owners of the property. Trustees have a legal duty to use the property as provided in the trust agreement and permitted by law. The beneficiaries retain what is known as **equitable title**, the right to benefit from the property as specified in the trust.

The grantor may retain control of the property. If you set up a revocable living trust with yourself as trustee, you retain the rights of ownership you'd have if the assets were still in your name. You can buy anything and add it to the trust, sell anything out of the trust, and give trust property to whomever you wish.

If you set up the trust by your will to take effect at your death—a **testamentary trust**—you retain ownership of the property during your lifetime, and on your death it passes to the trustee to be distributed to your beneficiaries as you designate.

We speak of putting assets "in" a trust, but they don't always change location. Certainly, a house does not. Stock certificates, on the other hand, would be delivered to the trustee to complete the transfer of assets to a trust.

It's helpful to think of a trust as an imaginary container. It's not a geographical place that protects your car, but a form of ownership that holds it for your benefit. On your car title, the

IF I MOVE AFTER SETTING UP A TRUST, WHICH STATE'S LAWS APPLY?

Trusts are governed by the law of the state in which they were established. Personal property in the trust, like a car or money or most other things, will be controlled by the trust. So will real property, but of course the real property will also be subject to the real property laws of the state in which it is located (i.e., regarding deeds and the like).

owner blank would simply read "the trustee of the Richard Petty Trust." It's common to put bank and brokerage accounts, as well as homes and other real estate, into a trust (and less common to put in cars because of potential liability and rapid depreciation).

After your trust comes into being, your assets will probably still be in the same place they were before you set it up—the car in the garage, the money in the bank, the land where it always was—but once the various assets have been transferred into the name of the trustee, they will have a different owner: the Richard Petty Trust, not Richard Petty.

This may sound abstract, but as this and the next chapter show, the benefits are concrete.

HOW DO TRUSTS OPERATE?

There is no such thing as a standard trust, just as there's no standard will. You can include any provision you want, as long as it doesn't conflict with state law or public policy. The provisions of a written trust instrument govern how the trustee holds and manages the property. That varies greatly, depending on why the trust was set up in the first place.

In a living trust, the grantor may be the trustee *and* the beneficiary. In trusts set up in your will, the trustee is often one or more persons or, for larger estates where investment expertise is required, a corporate trust company or bank.

Trust can be **revocable** (i.e., you can legally change the terms

KINDS OF TRUSTS

- **Charitable trusts** are created to support some charitable purpose. Often, these trusts will make an annual gift to a worthy cause of your choosing, simultaneously helping good causes and reducing the taxes on your estate.

- **Discretionary trusts** permit the trustee to distribute income and principal among various beneficiaries, or to control the disbursements to a single beneficiary, as he or she sees fit.

- **Insurance trusts** are tax-saving trusts in which trust assets are used to buy a life insurance policy whose proceeds benefit the grantor's beneficiaries (see chapter 8).

- **Living trusts** (see chapter 5) enable you to put your assets in a trust while still alive. You can wear all the hats—grantor, trustee, and beneficiary—or have someone else be trustee and have other beneficiaries.

- **Revocable trusts** are simply ones that can be changed, or even terminated, at any time by the grantor. Though most living trusts are revocable, a living trust and a revocable trust are not synonymous.

- **Irrevocable trusts** cannot be changed or terminated before the time specified in the trust, but the loss of flexibility may be offset by savings in taxes.

- **Spendthrift trusts** can be set up for people whom the grantor believes wouldn't be able to manage their own affairs—an extravagant relative or someone who's mentally incompetent. They may also be useful for beneficiaries who need protection from creditors.

- **Support trusts** direct the trustee to spend only as much income and principal as may be needed for the education and support of the beneficiary.

- **Testamentary trusts** are set up in wills.

- **Totten trusts** are not really trusts. They're a kind of bank account that passes to a beneficiary immediately upon your death.

- **Wealth trusts** are tax-saving trusts that benefit several generations of your descendants.

and end the trust) or **irrevocable**. Later chapters, particularly chapter 5, discuss the practical effects of each. Here it's enough to say that a revocable trust gives the donor great flexibility but no tax advantages or disadvantages. If the trust is revocable and you are the trustee, you will have to report the income from the trust on your personal income tax return (1040) instead of on a separate income tax statement for the trust (1041). The theory is that by retaining the right to terminate the trust, you have kept enough control of the property in it to treat it for tax purposes as if you owned it in your name.

Irrevocable trusts are the other side of the coin—far less flexible but the source of possible tax benefits. The trustee must file a separate tax return.

Trusts can be very simple, intended for limited purposes, or they can be quite complex, spanning two or more generations, providing tax benefits and protection from creditors of the beneficiary, and displacing a will as the primary estate-planning vehicle.

WHO NEEDS A TRUST?

Parents with Young Children

If you have young children, want to assure a good education for them, and know that there will be enough assets to do so after your death (including life insurance proceeds), you should consider setting up a trust. The trustee manages the property in the trust for the benefit of your children during their lifetime or until they reach the ages that you designate. Then, any remaining property in the trust may be divided among the children. This type of arrangement has an obvious advantage over an inflexible division of property among children of different ages without regard to their respective ages or needs. Trusts are more flexible than giving outright gifts to minors in your will, which requires a guardian, or a gift under the Uniform Transfers to Minors Act, which requires appointment of a custodian and transfers of property to the child at age eighteen. These are some issues to consider when setting up a trust for the benefit of your children:

- **One trust or many?** Most people will set up one trust that all the children can draw on until they've completed their educations (or reached an age by which they should have done so). Then, the remaining principal is divided among them equally. This permits the trustee greater flexibility to distribute ("sprinkle") the money unequally according to need; for example, one child may choose to pursue an advanced degree at an expensive private university while another may drop out of community college after a semester. Obviously, they will have different educational expenses.

Where very young children are involved, it's especially important to build in some flexibility; who knows if a two-year-old may turn out to need special counseling or education by the time he turns five or six?

There are two philosophies about what to do if there's a disparity in ages among the children. One theory is that the older children have already received the benefit of the parents' spending before they died, so the trustee should have authority to make unequal distributions in favor of the younger children to compensate. The other camp, by contrast, thinks it better to establish separate.trusts, so that the older children don't have to wait until they're well into adulthood before the trust assets are distributed (which usually happens when the youngest child reaches the age of majority). You'll have to decide which course is best for your family's circumstances.

Generally speaking, the less money you have to distribute, the more likely you would put it all in one trust. Since there is a limited amount of money, you want to pool it to be sure that it goes for the greatest need. (An exception would be when the children are grown; you'd probably want separate trusts even if the trust assets were small.) On the other hand, if equality is your primary consideration and there's plenty of money available to take care of each child's likely needs, then you may want to set up separate trusts even for each minor child, to assure that each gets an equal share.

- **What should the assets be used for?** You can specify that the trust pay for education, health care, food, rent, and other basic support. Given life's unpredictability, however, it's often better to write a vague standard (e.g., "for the support of my children") into the document and allow the trustee the discretion to decide if an expenditure is legitimate. Such a provision also gives the trustee flexibility. For example, if one of your children has an unanticipated expenditure, like a serious illness, the trustee could give him more money that year than the other children.

• **When should the assets be distributed?** Some parents pick the age of majority (eighteen) or the age when a child will be out of college (twenty-two or so). If all the assets are in one trust that serves several children, you would usually have the assets distributed when the youngest child reaches the target age. If you have separate trusts and a pretty good idea about each child's level of maturity, you can pick the age that seems appropriate for each to receive his or her windfall.

If you don't know when each child will be capable of handling money, you can leave the age of distribution up to the trustee (and risk friction between the trustee and the children), have the trustee distribute the assets at different times (say, half when the first child turns twenty-five and the rest when the youngest does so), or just pick an age for each child, such as thirty.

Like any trust, a children's trust costs money to set up: lawyers' fees for creating the trust, fees for preparing and filing the separate tax returns required, and so on. For families with limited assets, it might be best to give the money via a custodial account under the Uniform Gifts to Minors Act or the Uniform Transfers to Minors Act (see chapter 6).

People with Beneficiaries Who Need Help

Trusts are especially popular among people with beneficiaries who aren't able to manage property well. This includes elderly beneficiaries with special needs or a relative who may be untrustworthy with money. If you have a granddaughter who has been in a juvenile detention center, for example, it may be a good idea to require her to obtain money from a trustee who would exercise discretion about whether to distribute it to her, instead of giving her a gift outright in your will. A **discretionary**

trust gives the trustee leeway to give the beneficiary as much or as little he or she thinks appropriate.

Another type of trust, for improvident beneficiaries, is a **spendthrift trust**. It's simply a trust in which your instructions to the trustee carefully control how much money is released from the trust and at what intervals, so you can keep an irresponsible beneficiary from getting thousands of dollars in one stroke. You can stipulate that the trustee will pay only certain expenses for the beneficiary—those you (or the trustee) consider legitimate, such as rent and utility bills. In spendthrift trusts, beneficiaries cannot assign their interest in the trust, meaning they cannot transfer their rights to someone else (say, in return for cash). Creditors of beneficiaries can't get any portion of the principal in a trust to satisfy a debt but can make a claim (if it's otherwise legal) on whatever income the beneficiary receives from the trust. Spendthrift provisions raise a number of tricky questions and should be used cautiously—your lawyer can tell you whether such a trust is right for your situation.

People Who Own Hard-to-Divide Property

Trusts help you transfer property that's not easy to divide evenly among several beneficiaries. Suppose you have a little vacation cottage on the Cape and four children who each want to use it. You can pass it to them in a trust that sets out each child's right to use the property, establishes procedures to prevent conflicts, requires that when the property is sold the trustee divide the proceeds evenly (or unevenly, if some children aren't as well off as others), and sets up a procedure by which any child may buy out another's interest in the cottage.

People Who Want to Control Their Property

Through a trust, you can maintain more control over a gift than you can through a will. Some people use trusts to pass on money to a relative when they have doubts about that person's spouse. For example, you love your son but don't trust his wife, Livia. You're afraid she'll spend the money you give him on astrologers and shoes. Leave the money in trust for your son instead of making a direct gift to him. You can direct that he get

SOME REASONS TO HAVE A TRUST

1. *Trusts can be flexible; you can authorize that payments fluctuate with the cost of living, allow extra withdrawals in case of emergency, or even set a standard figure for payment each year; if the income doesn't meet that amount, the difference can be made up out of the principal.*

2. *On the other hand, a trust can be structured so that it imposes discipline on the beneficiary. You could require the beneficiary to live within a set figure, getting a certain amount of income each year regardless of inflation, need, or the stock market's effect on the principal.*

3. *A trust is sometimes set up in divorce to provide for the education of the couple's children.*

4. *A trust can also be helpful if you want to make a major charitable gift but wish to retain some use of the gift.*

only the income, so neither he nor his wife can squander the principal. Furthermore, in many states if you leave money in trust to your son, Livia can't get at the assets if they divorce.

People Concerned About Estate Taxes

Trusts are very useful to people with substantial assets because they can help avoid or reduce estate taxes. For example, by establishing an appropriate kind of trust for your children's benefit you can make tax-free gifts (up to the limit allowed by law) each year to them or your grandchildren during your lifetime, even if they're minors. This will reduce your taxable estate and save taxes upon your death. A properly drawn trust may also reduce estate taxes by utilizing the marital deduction or avoiding the generation skipping tax (see chapter 8).

SETTING UP A TRUST

If you establish a trust in your will, its provisions are contained in the will. If you create a trust directly, its provisions are contained in the **trust agreement** or **trust declaration**. The provisions of that trust document (not your will or state law) will determine what happens to the property in the trust upon your death.

With any type of trust, one of the most important issues is choosing the trustee. See chapter 10 for a discussion of this issue.

Funding the Trust

A testamentary trust is funded after your death with assets that you've specified in your will and through beneficiary designations of your life insurance, IRA, etc. Such trusts generally receive most of the estate's assets, such as the proceeds from the sale of a house. Or you could set up an "unfunded" standby trust. This is a trust that could be called "minimally" funded to avoid confusion. It may have a nominal sum of money in it— $100 or so—to get it started while you're alive (and thus make it a living trust), but it only receives substantial assets when you die. Your pourover will would direct that many or all of your assets be transferred from your estate to the trust at your death. Making your life insurance payable to the trust, as well as designating the trust as the beneficiary of IRAs, profit-sharing plans, and so on, will pass these assets directly to the trust. They won't have to go through probate. However, other assets not already owned by the trust when you die will have to go through probate. This is why many lawyers shy away from unfunded trusts. (But see chapter 11 for some reasons why you might want your estate to go through probate.)

If your estate—with life insurance benefits included—will add up to more than $1 million, you can save taxes by removing the life insurance proceeds from your estate and establishing an irrevocable life insurance trust that owns the policy; all **incidents of ownership** in the policy (see page 116) belong to the trust. When you die, the insurance proceeds are paid into the trust, escaping estate taxation and creditors.

Trusts and Taxes

Chapter 8 discusses death and taxes, and trusts are a major part of that discussion. However, there are a few basic principles worth mentioning here. While gifts under the $1 million level (in a trust or in a will) escape federal *estate tax*, the recipients of the trust income will still have to pay *income tax* when they receive income from the trust. They would not have to pay tax on the principal in the trust when they collect it (unless their state has an inheritance tax).

The trustee pays, out of the principal, the taxes on income from the trust that's reinvested or put back into the principal. Capital gains from the sale of stock, real estate, and the like are generally added to the principal, unless you specify otherwise.

The choice of trustee can affect the tax the trust owes. If the beneficiary is made the only trustee, some of the tax advantages of the trust can be lost. Similarly, the more powers the grantor retains, the more likely the assets in the trust will be taxable to the grantor either during the grantor's lifetime as income tax or after death in the grantor's estate. Consult your attorney or a tax adviser before setting up any trust for tax purposes.

TERMINATING A TRUST

Only charitable trusts can last indefinitely. Because they accomplish a substantial benefit to the public, it is entirely appropriate that Rhodes scholarships, Pulitzer and Nobel prizes, and thousands of other awards and grants be funded by trusts that are expected to endure.

Private trusts—set up to benefit private beneficiaries—cannot last forever. The **rule against perpetuities**, which is embodied in state law and may vary somewhat from state to state, is designed to limit the time a trust may be operative. Usually it specifies that a trust can last no longer than the lifetime of a beneficiary alive at the time the trust is created, plus twenty-one years. So if you set up a trust to benefit your infant granddaughter and any children she may eventually have, and she has a long life, your trust may extend a hundred years, but not much more.

Your trust agreement should contain a clause that provides for how it can be terminated. A good trust drawn up by a lawyer will certainly have such a clause.

A trust often terminates when the principal is distributed to the beneficiaries, at the time stated in the trust agreement. For example, you might provide that a trust for the benefit of your children would end when the youngest child reaches a certain age. At that time, the trustee would distribute the assets to the beneficiaries according to your instructions. The law generally allows a "windup phase" to complete administration of trust duties (e.g., filing tax returns) after the trust has officially terminated.

You can also give your trustees the discretion to distribute the trust assets and terminate the trust when they think it's a good idea, or place some restrictions on their ability to do so. For example, you could allow the trustees to terminate the trust at their discretion, provided that your daughter has completed her education.

Your trust should have a termination provision even if it is an irrevocable trust. "Irrevocability" means that you, the grantor, can't change your mind about how you want the trust to terminate. You cannot terminate the trust yourself and get your property back. It doesn't mean that you can't set up termination procedures in the first place, however.

If you have an irrevocable trust and don't have a termination provision, it can usually terminate only if all beneficiaries consent and no material purpose of the trust is defeated. However, an irrevocable trust can also be terminated if there was fraud, duress, undue influence, or other problems when the trust was set up; if the trustee and the beneficiary become the same person; if the operation of the trust becomes impracticable or illegal; or if the period of time specified in state law expires. We're obviously into technical territory here, so the basic rule is, don't set up an irrevocable trust unless you're prepared to live—and die—by its terms.

CHAPTER FIVE

■

Living Trusts

A LIVING TRUST—an **inter vivos trust**, if you want to be formal—allows you to put your assets in a trust while you're still alive. If your living trust is revocable, as almost all are, it gives you great flexibility. You or someone in whom you have confidence manages the property, usually for the benefit of you or your family. Most people name themselves as trustees and find there is no difference between managing the trust and managing their own property—they have the right to buy, sell, or give property as before, though the property is in the trust's name rather than their own.

A living trust is one of the two main ways to avoid probate (the other being joint tenancy or survivorship). One of the purposes of probate is to determine the disposition of the property you leave at death. Since the trustee of your living trust owns that property—either someone you named while alive or someone you chose to succeed you as trustee at your death—there is no need for probate.

Living trusts have become extremely popular in recent years. Even though a living trust is a useful, simple, and relatively inexpensive way to plan your estate, it does not magically solve all your problems.

For example, as states have simplified their probate procedures, many of the advantages of living trusts have diminished. And though they're great for some people, you can't assume they're great for you.

Deciding whether a living trust is right for you depends on

the size of your estate, what kinds of assets it contains, and what plans you have for yourself and your family.

SHOULD YOU HAVE A LIVING TRUST?

The debate over living trusts has often focused on controlling costs and avoiding probate, but many lawyers think this misses the far more significant features of living trusts.

The living trust, while offering advantages over probate, isn't guaranteed to save you money. If your records are well organized, your assets are simple (not necessarily small, just easily identified), your beneficiaries aren't contentious, your state has inexpensive probate procedures for estates of your size, and your probate court and lawyer are efficient, legal costs of probate might be so low that it costs less to pass the property through a will than via a living trust. Besides, since you should have a will even if you do use a living trust, you'll be paying some court fees anyhow, even though most of your property will be controlled by the living trust. And it might be possible to use other probate-avoidance techniques—joint tenancy, pay-on-death accounts, life insurance, and others mentioned in chapter 2—that don't entail the costs of a living trust.

You may want to determine how much probate will cost your estate and compare it to the costs, financial and otherwise, of a living trust for the same size estate. An easy way to decide whether a living trust is right for you is to show your lawyer your list of assets (see appendix) and ask if, given all the circumstances, a living trust will save you money.

However, don't forget the many situations more important than any cost savings. For example, the advantage to an older or ill person is that a living trust avoids an expensive and undesirable court proceeding to select a court-appointed guardian or conservator.

Here are two other examples of how a living trust can help.

Mary is a widow, without children or any close relatives. She is no longer able to live alone in her home or to handle her finances. She transfers her property and other assets to a trustee, who will sell the house and invest the proceeds along with the other assets, under a revocable trust, to provide for Mary's support during her lifetime and to dispose of the assets after her death to the people or charitable organizations she designates. Should Mary change her mind as to any of them or should an old friend for whom she had provided a gift die, Mary can make a simple amendment to the trust by a written letter or memo signed by her and delivered to the trustee. No witnesses are necessary.

John is a doctor in his early forties. He resides with his wife, Jane, and their five children, ages two, four, six, eight, and ten (with expectation of more) in their home. He has a good income from his practice and is gradually building up an estate. However, in the event of his death or disability, he would not be able to provide the desired support for his family. He is able to purchase a large life insurance policy. By creating a declaration of trust or revocable trust agreement with himself and Jane as trustees, and with a trust company or individual as successor trustee, and providing that the proceeds of the life insurance policy be payable to the trustees, John can provide for the support of Jane and the support and education of the children. Even if Jane also passes away while they are still minors, the successor trustee will have ample funds to provide for the children.

Requirements for setting up a living trust vary with each state. In general, you execute a document that states that you're creating a trust to hold property for the benefit of yourself and your family, or whomever you want it to benefit. Some trust declarations list the major assets (home, investments) that you're putting in trust; others refer to another document (a **schedule**) in which you list the exact property that will begin the trust. Or you may transfer the property to the trustee under a trust agreement. In any case, you must be certain that the transfer of property is actually made. A list of items in the trust or a schedule is not enough unless the wording of the trust or bills of sale or deeds to the trustee actually convey the property.

You can add and subtract property whenever you wish. You will have to change the ownership registration on whatever property you put into the trust—deeds, stocks, bonds, brokerage accounts, bank accounts, etc.—from your own name to the name of the trust (e.g., the John A. Smith Trust). If you make yourself the trustee, you will have to remember to sign yourself in transactions as "John A. Smith, Trustee," instead of using your name only.

When you transfer property into a living trust, the trustee becomes its owner, which is why you must transfer title to the property from your own name to that of the trustee. But you retain the right to use and enjoy the property, and because you do, in the cold eyes of the tax authorities the property in the trust belongs to you, the grantor, for tax purposes. If you receive income from the assets, you must still report the income from the trust directly on your income tax return. The trust itself often files a separate income tax statement as well, though the IRS doesn't require one if the grantor and trustee are the same person. You can apply to the Internal Revenue Service for an employer identification number (EIN) for the trust.

You can make anyone you want the trustee. You can also name a **successor trustee** to take over in the event of the original trustee's death, incapacity, or resignation.

In a revocable living trust, you keep the right to manage your property whether you're the trustee or not, since you have a right to change the terms of the trust, the trustee, and the property in the trust at any time. When you die, your successor trustee distributes the property according to the terms of the trust. The successor trustee can be your spouse or an adult child or any other person, but you can name a bank or trust company if you are willing to have their fees paid from the trust (see chapter 10 for more information).

A living trust can continue long after you die. If you want the trust to benefit your infant grandchildren, for example, you can specify that the trustee make distributions to them as needed until they have reached specified ages. Living trusts, like wills, give you wide flexibility in distributing your property. For example, the trust agreement could say "at my death, my trustee is to give my car to my son Cain, my coat to my son Jacob," and so on. Your instructions can tell the trustee to continue managing assets for the benefit of someone else, distribute them to any beneficiaries you choose, or perform some combination of these actions. If beneficiaries of your living trust die before you do, the property reverts to you unless you've named other people (**contingent beneficiaries**) for those gifts.

If taxes aren't a worry—and they won't be in the vast majority of estates—you should be sure to retain the right to revoke or amend your trust whenever you wish (see chapter 9 for more about this). Have your lawyer create a revocable trust agreement, which allows you to change the terms or trustee.

It can be a bother to set up and fund the living trust, but the payoff for your family comes when you die. If Ilda wanted her property to go to her friend Rick, for example, she would put it in a trust and name him co-trustee or successor trustee as well as beneficiary. Then, when she dies, he becomes sole trustee and acting in that capacity transfers the trust property to the beneficiary—himself. Since the property does not have to go through probate, there's no break in continuity, no court involvement, fewer delays, and little or no expense (though there is work— like any executor, Rick would have duties gathering assets, paying bills and taxes, etc.).

A living trust can contain other, separate trusts, which gives you a nice flexibility. For example, if you plan to leave some of your property to your minor children in trust (see chapter 6), you could specify in your trust that the children's property goes into a separate, irrevocable children's trust. You can design separate trusts for several beneficiaries, all funded (usually at your death) by the assets in your living trust.

OTHER ADVANTAGES

• **Helps in managing your affairs.** If you have a trustee, a living trust can manage your property. Say you rent out condos; your trustee can take over the management while you receive the income (minus the trustee's fees).

A living trust can also provide a way to care for you and your property in case you become disabled, which is why many people use them. You'd typically set up a revocable living trust, fund it adequately (or give someone in whom you have confidence power of attorney to fund it in the event of your incapacity), and name a reliable alternative trustee (often an adult child) to manage it should you become ill. This avoids the delay and red tape of expensive, court-ordered guardianship. And at the same time, the trustee can take over any duties you had of providing for other family members.

• **Protects your privacy.** Like all trusts, living trusts maintain the deceased's privacy more than wills since there's usually no public record required. However, if the trust is funded through a pourover provision in your will, the items transferred from your probate estate may appear in a public record, especially if the will is contested. And in some states if you put certain kinds of property in the trust, such as real estate, securities, or a safe-deposit box, you may have to register the trust, which creates a public record of its contents. You may be able to get around this requirement through use of a **nominee partnership** (see below).

• **Easy to create and change.** For most simple estates, it's not that hard for a lawyer to create a living trust tailored to your

BY ANY OTHER NAME

In law, many words are "terms of art": They have special legal meanings. However, in talking about trusts, you find a bewildering array of names, some of which refer to the same kind of entity. In part this is because trusts are generally governed by the diverse laws of fifty states and the federal government, in part because lawyers (and authors) often make up their own names for various clever trusts that take advantage of changes in the law. So don't worry if you go to a lawyer and you've never heard of the kind of trust he or she is talking about (or vice versa). What matters is how it works, not what it's called.

estate's objectives, and you don't have to go through the formalities required to execute or change wills. Some states require that your living trust be registered with the state, but that's a simple procedure. Most states require no witnesses or other legal language to execute the living trust or an amendment to it: Just have your lawyer write it—or do it yourself, though that can be risky (see below)—and sign your name.

• **Greater control of assets.** In some states, a spouse cannot take an elective share in the trust assets (see the discussion of **taking against the will** in chapter 7), making a living trust a way of disinheriting a spouse in these jurisdictions.

• **Good for far-flung family and assets.** Say you want your estate administered by someone who doesn't live in your state, such as a child who's grown up and moved away. A living trust might be better than a will because the trustee probably won't have to meet the residency requirements some state laws impose upon executors.

If you have property in another state, many lawyers recommend setting up a living trust to hold the title to that property. This helps you avoid time-consuming, complicated ancillary probate procedures, since trusts are governed by the law of the state in which they were created and the property will not have

WHAT A LIVING TRUST WON'T DO

A living trust is obviously an important estate-planning tool. In recent years, many people have come to expect them to work wonders. Here's a list of miracles they won't perform.

1. **Won't help you avoid taxes.** *A revocable living trust doesn't save any income or estate taxes that couldn't also be saved by a properly prepared will. The property in the revocable living trust is still counted as part of your taxes. Your successor trustee still has to pay income taxes generated by trust property and owed at your death. (Your executor would have to pay such taxes out of your estate if you had disposed of the property by a will instead of a trust.) And if the estate is large enough to trigger state and federal estate or inheritance taxes, your successor trustee has to file the appropriate returns. These and other duties can make the cost of administering some estates distributed by living trusts almost as high as traditional estate administration.*

     You may be able to avoid or lower taxes by using one of the tax-saving trusts briefly discussed in chapter 8. But a simple revocable living trust by itself will not save or increase taxes.

2. **Won't make a will unnecessary.** *You still need a simple will to take care of assets you fail to transfer to the trust or that you acquire shortly before your death. If you have minor children, you probably need a will to appoint a guardian for them.*

3. **Won't affect nonprobate assets.** *Like a will, a living trust won't control the disposition of jointly owned property, life insurance payable to a beneficiary, or other nonprobate property (see chapter 2).*

to go through probate. However, you'll have to have a lawyer in the state where the property is located prepare a deed conveying the property from you to the trust. Then, when you die, your trustee can simply have a deed executed to the beneficiaries of your trust. The property won't have to go through probate.

4. **Won't protect your assets from creditors.** *Creditors can attach living trust assets. In fact, the assets you put in a living trust don't have a probate administration and thus lose the protection of the statute of limitations—your creditors may have longer to get at them. And your family doesn't receive the* **family allowance** *granted for a probate estate, which sets aside a certain amount of money for family support that takes priority over creditors' claims. An irrevocable trust can help shield your assets from creditors, but this involves complicated legal provisions that require a lawyer's advice. And, of course, you lose control over the assets.*

5. **Won't protect your assets absolutely from disgruntled heirs.** *While it is harder to challenge a living trust than a will, a relative can still bring suit in trial court to challenge a living trust on the grounds of lack of mental capacity, undue influence, duress, or for other reasons.*

6. **Won't entirely eliminate delays.** *A living trust might well lessen the time it takes to distribute your assets after you die, but it won't completely eliminate delays. Many state laws impose a waiting period for creditors to file claims against estates with living trusts. The period usually isn't as long as the time required to probate a will but it can stretch into several months. The trustee will still have to collect debts owed to your estate after you die, prepare tax returns, and pay bills and distribute assets just like an executor would. All that takes time. In addition, there may not be hardships caused by delays if you leave your property in a will. In most states, the assets of an estate are available to the executor quickly after the testator's death, so your family could probably get enough money to live on soon after you die.*

DISADVANTAGES

- **Cost.** While a lawyer isn't required for setting up a revocable living trust, it's usually a good idea to hire one. Though there may be some eventual savings in reduced or eliminated probate costs, registration fees and other incidental costs of the trust are incurred up front, while the savings generally don't accrue until your death.

- **Title problems.** Not all items may be easily transferred into a trust. Jewelry can be a problem, and if you transfer title to your car into the trust, you may have trouble getting insurance on it since you don't own it anymore. Check with your insurance agent.

- **Tax problems.** The federal estate tax allows an estate to use a fiscal year, other than a calendar year, as the "taxable year" used in tax deadlines. Trusts don't receive the same flexibility. Each trust must use a calendar year. If you have a large estate and timing is a consideration, it might save you money to pass your assets via a will instead of a trust. You don't have to have a separate taxpayer ID number for a living trust, but trusts are required to make estimated tax payments, while estates are exempt from this requirement for the first two years. There may be state tax considerations, too: Maryland, for example, charges income taxes on trusts but not estates. Check your state law for such traps before setting up a living trust.

- **Less protection.** A trust administration is not an estate administration and you do not have the protection of the claims period, nor are you already in probate court with an expedited way for the court to settle disputes over construction of documents or issues of facts regarding status of beneficiaries. If those issues are to be determined by the court in the trust administration, a separate **cause of action** (claim in law and fact to support a valid lawsuit) needs to be filed with a **summons** (notice to parties), related costs, and time delay. In contentious situations, an estate administration may be advisable.

- **Other traps.** In some states, revocable trusts (along with other nonprobate transfers like insurance policies) are not automatically revoked or amended on divorce, unlike wills. If you don't amend the trust, your ex could end up being the beneficiary. (See chapter 9 and "Splitting Up: Divorce and Remarriage" in chapter 7.)

If you're in certain specialized situations, you might ask your lawyer whether a living trust is a good idea: If not properly drafted, it can jeopardize Medicaid qualifications and possibly make any land received via the trust subject to laws pertaining to toxic waste cleanup. Depending on the state in which the property is located, putting your home in a revocable trust might jeopardize a homestead exemption, might require a transfer fee, or might cause your property to be reevaluated for property tax purposes.

Finally, though a living trust you write while residing in one state generally remains valid if you move to another, it's a good idea to check with a lawyer familiar with the statutes of your new state to see whether the trust should be revised to account for differences in the law, especially if you're moving from a community property state to a common-law state or vice versa.

PRACTICAL STEPS IN SETTING UP A LIVING TRUST

Who should advise you about living trusts? Your lawyer is an obvious choice. Your bank might be another alternative for setting up a trust. Most banks now make available a living trust service in which the bank manages and invests the money you put in the trust, and you have the right to change or terminate the trust at any time. Though there often is no setup charge, the bank's management charge can add up, maybe even exceeding the cost of probate. It all depends on your estate and your bank.

For people with substantial assets, or people who don't want the uncertainty and work of writing and funding their own trust or the possibility of costly errors in doing so, it's best to use a lawyer. It's especially good to have a lawyer's help in figuring out which assets to put in the living trust and which to put elsewhere and leave for disposition via your will. By providing money-saving advice like this, lawyers often save more than they charge in legal fees.

By doing some preparation, you can minimize the time the lawyer spends on setting up the trust and reduce your legal costs.

SAVE YOUR LAWYER TIME . . . AND YOURSELF MONEY

Your involvement shouldn't stop after the trust document is executed. In a living trust, someone must then take charge of funding (transferring assets into) the trust. This can involve changing car titles, executing deeds or bills of sale, reregistering stocks, and so on. Some lawyers describe the often onerous process as "going through probate before you die." Usually you don't want to pay a lawyer's hourly fee to undertake these sorts of routine clerical tasks. Sometimes lawyers will delegate them to their paralegals, who will charge you less, but it still costs you money. On the other hand, lawyers complain that clients often (and understandably) neglect this tedious process after they walk out of the office with an elegantly crafted revocable living trust in hand. If disaster strikes, much of the estate still has to go through probate because you failed to complete the funding process.

What to do? If you're short on money, long on time (as many retired people are), have few assets that need retitling, or are certain you're willing to do the legwork, then do it yourself. Or you and a paralegal could split up the work, with the lawyer supervising the process by checking with you a few times after the trust is executed. Because of the vagaries of real estate law, many lawyers may want to take care of transferring real property themselves.

As with making a will, you should ask your lawyer what documents you should bring with you. After collecting all the needed records, deeds, bank statements, etc., make a list of what you have and where you want it to go when you die.

A lawyer's fee for preparing a living trust might be somewhat higher than that for preparing a simple will, but you may save money in the long run by avoiding probate costs.

Special Considerations

When you write your living trust, make sure you consider these issues:

• **Coordinated estate plan.** It's important to make sure to coordinate the trust with the rest of your estate plan. The executor of your will still must pay income and inheritance taxes and various probate expenses, but if too many of the estate assets are in the trust, he or she may not have enough money to do so. One way to meet this contingency is to give the trustee (and successor) power to make these payments from trust assets.

- **Coordinated disability plan.** Most lawyers will help you plan for your possible incapacity. Sometimes they'll draft a durable power of attorney (see chapter 12) to go with the revocable trust, which will give your **attorney in fact** (the person you've selected to act for you) the power to receive assets from and transfer assets to the trust in case you become incompetent. In many (perhaps most) cases, the attorney in fact will also be a co-trustee; both are often your spouse, especially in smaller estates. The conditions placed on the power will vary depending on your family and financial situation.

However, when different people are carrying out those functions, lawyers caution not to give the attorney in fact actual control over the trust; that limitation is written into the power of attorney. The reason: It sets up a potential conflict of interest between one family member who's charged with looking out for your benefit and another, perhaps more distant, relative who stands to benefit from the trust. That person would have a vested interest in keeping more of the money in the trust, even though you might need it to pay for, say, a better nursing home.

Finally, in states where they are allowed, your lawyer will probably prepare and coordinate a living will or health-care power of attorney (see chapter 12) with your living trust.

- **One trust or two?** In most cases, it works fine for a couple to use one living trust for all their shared property, whether in a community property state or common-law state. Most couples prefer to keep ownership of important assets shared. That way, you don't have to worry about dividing part-ownership of various assets (e.g., his 50 percent share of the house goes into his trust, hers into her trust). Nor, in the event of marital discord, does one spouse have to worry that the other's trust owns their house.

Such a joint marital trust will commonly provide that the property of the first spouse to die will go to his beneficiaries upon his death. Since most of his property will likely go to the surviving spouse, it winds up back in the living trust anyway combined with her property. (When tax considerations come into play, this might change.)

Remember, such a setup transfers the property to the other spouse with no conditions of any kind. Also remember that in some states, divorce does not automatically invalidate a living trust. If you want to maintain more control over your property after you die, talk to your lawyer.

- **Revocable or irrevocable?** As with other trusts, living trusts can be revocable (changeable) or irrevocable. Most living trusts are revocable. But some people (usually those with a lot of money) do use irrevocable living trusts to avoid taxes; you give up control over the assets in the trust in return for escaping some estate, income, or gift taxes. They're usually used to give money to charity (**charitable remainder trusts**).

An irrevocable trust doesn't avoid taxes entirely—it merely sets up a separate taxable entity that might be able to pay taxes at a lower rate than if all the assets were combined in one estate. It can also offer a bit more protection from creditors.

If you make the trust irrevocable to reduce taxes and avoid creditors, prepare for a lot of paperwork. And understand that you lose the flexibility of a revocable living trust. Be sure to consult a lawyer before setting up an irrevocable trust.

Funding the Living Trust

Setting up the trust is actually the easy part; the hard part is putting something in it—what's called "funding the trust." This includes not just depositing money in the trust account but also transferring title of assets to the name of the trustee.

Living trusts can be funded now, while you're living, or after you are dead. If you want to fund it before you die (a **funded trust**), you transfer title to your assets to the trustee and make the trustee the owner of any newly acquired assets you want to go into the trust. Any assets in the trust will avoid probate. The more you leave out, the more involved probate will be.

How do you transfer titles to the trustee? You have to reregister title documents—for example, transfer title of your bank accounts and stocks to the trustee's name and prepare and sign a new deed to your house designating the trustee as owner. If you have any doubts about how to proceed, consult your lawyer. Make sure to keep a record of these transfers; it will make your successor trustee's job easier when you die.

Some lawyers recommend the use of a **nominee partnership** to avoid certain problems of funding a living trust. Instead of putting the assets in the name of the trust, you put the assets in the name of a partnership that doesn't own the property but does retain control over its use. The partners are usually the trustees of the living trust. Such an arrangement is sometimes preferable for banks and businesses that prefer to deal with partnerships instead of trustees. If your trust will be involved in a lot of business transactions, ask your lawyer if a nominee partnership arrangement would be useful.

What should you leave out? The special tax treatment given IRAs might encourage you to leave them in your name. The fees your state charges to transfer title of a mortgage or other property increase the cost of transfer, so you might consider leaving them out.

Some people are just afraid to take the family house out of the husband's and wife's names in joint tenancy and put it into a living trust in the name of one of the spouses. Maybe that's because then they won't own their house (the trust will) or because they don't trust the spouse who is to be trustee to hold and manage it for the benefit of both spouses. In such cases, a lawyer may suggest putting the living trust in both your names, for example, "the James and Ima Hogg Trust," instead of just one name; both spouses are co-trustees. If you leave the family home out of the trust and in joint tenancy, remember that it will go through probate upon the death of the surviving spouse.

If the trust is in one name only, and the other spouse is not a co- or successor trustee, many lawyers recommend leaving one checking account with ample funds out of the living trust and not have it poured over into the trust when that person dies. This is as much for psychological as financial reasons, since it reassures the spouse who is not a trustee that he or she will have access to funds upon the death of the other. The checking account should be in the name of both spouses. That way, if one dies, the other will have the right to write checks on the account. It will go through probate, but if both spouses had access to it, there should be little delay in getting money. Or, if your state allows it, you may want to use a **pay-on-death** bank account to avoid probate (the pros and cons are discussed in chapter 2).

Finally, keeping a few assets out of the living trust can help protect against creditors' claims down the line. When your estate contains some property and goes through probate, it triggers the running of the statute of limitations on claims against your entire estate. Creditors are put on notice that you have died, and once the statutory period runs out, the estate is safe from most claims. If, on the other hand, everything you had was in the living trust and there was no probate, the time within which a creditor could come after the estate might be extended.

The important point: Be sure to go through each of your assets with your lawyer to determine whether it's wise to transfer that asset to the trust.

The Unfunded Living Trust

The other way to fund a trust is to have the assets transferred to it just before you die or after your death.

Many people choose to fund trusts through their wills. To do this, you set up a revocable trust and a pourover will, which transfers the assets into the trust upon your death. You can add some assets to the trust before you die, but generally the will would specify that all estate property would pour over into the trust, including life insurance and other death benefits.

Obviously, you can't avoid probate this way. So who would use this approach? Maybe people who don't want to go through the hassle of funding a living trust while they're alive, but also don't want their after-death gifts to be a matter of record. They could give their estate to a trust via their will, and specify named beneficiaries through the privacy of the trust.

The other option is to have it funded when you're facing death or disability. You give someone (often, your lawyer, spouse, or friend; see chapter 12) a durable power of attorney. Then, if you should become disabled, that person has the authority to fund the trust and transfer assets into it. Since that person is either a trustee or an alternative trustee, he or she can use the assets to care for you in your final illness.

Many lawyers caution against trying to fund unfunded trusts at the last minute. Your state may not allow granting such powers of attorney. If you should die before you or your trustee can transfer your assets into an unfunded trust (a process that can take weeks), then those assets will go through probate as your will pours them over to the trust. All in all, you're better off funding the trust when it is created.

CHAPTER SIX

■

Common Estate-Planning Situations

WITH THE BASICS of will and trusts in mind, how might you use these devices in planning your estate? This chapter sets out the most common considerations, focusing on "typical" married couples of various kinds. The next chapter will discuss estate planning for people who don't fit these common patterns. Keep in mind that this discussion applies to people who die with estates worth less than $1 million, the present level at which the federal estate tax takes effect.

GENERAL CONSIDERATIONS FOR MARRIED COUPLES

While no two marriages are alike, most married couples share some basic estate-planning needs, some of which are outlined below. What's more critical than the specifics that appear here, however, is that you discuss these matters with your partner. Often, couples will arrive at a lawyer's office only to discover that they have different fears and desires about where their money should go after they die. The husband might want some of his property to go to the couple's grown children, to help them get started in life. The wife, on the other hand, might see the limited job market for herself and want more of his money to go to support her. These are intimate matters that will have to be hammered out between you and your partner—preferably before you talk to a lawyer.

When you get married, you should be sure to rewrite your will or at least modify it by codicil. In some states, a will is **revoked** (that is, canceled) by marriage, unless the will expressly declares that it was executed in contemplation of that particular marriage and that it shall not be revoked by that marriage. In all states, the law provides that your spouse can take a share of your estate, no matter what your will says (see next chapter). You'll want to factor that into your estate plan and may want to alter your will to account for it.

Most married couples with modest estates (and that's by far the majority of them) will execute simple wills in which each partner leaves everything to the surviving spouse. This is especially true if the couple is past the prime earning years or if one spouse has depended on the other for support, and the children are grown and earning money.

A married couple's estate plan will usually change over time: they accumulate more assets, children are born and then leave the household, and the chances diminish that one spouse will long outlive the other. Here are some considerations for both young and middle-aged couples, assuming that one or both spouses work outside the home and that together they have a middle class income.

Younger Couples

Marianne and Gilligan are in their thirties. They are concerned about things like taking care of their minor children if they both die and making sure there's money set aside to pay for college (see next section), and, if one of them dies, giving the other an adequate income.

Because they haven't paid off their house, they bought mortgage-canceling insurance. For their other debts, they've arranged a debt-payment schedule and life insurance plan so their children won't be burdened with this duty if they die soon. They haven't yet earned enough money to worry about estate tax planning.

For all these reasons, they need a relatively simple basic will that leaves everything to the surviving spouse. The principal goal is to protect the surviving partner, who may have several decades to live if the other dies unexpectedly. Passing the property by will avoids the complications and limited income of an irrevocable marital trust, which would give the surviving spouse only the income from the assets, not the assets themselves. In addition, they made each other beneficiary of their respective life insurance policies and other benefit plans.

This estate plan and will are interim documents, which Marianne and Gilligan will update as their assets and incomes grow.

Thurston and Lovey, on the other hand, have substantial assets, including a family business. Their plan includes a marital revocable living trust that leaves the surviving spouse the family assets. This will avoid probate, which is likely to be more complicated and costly for a larger estate than a simple one. They also have life insurance to provide liquid assets. Finally, each also has a will that leaves the residue of the estate to the trust; that will pick up any assets somehow left out of the trust.

Both couples have health-care powers of attorney, which lets each spouse make decisions for the other if either becomes incapacitated, and a living will. These are discussed in chapter 12.

Neither Marianne and Gilligan nor Thurston and Lovey uses a reciprocal power of attorney. Young couples (whose marriages are statistically most likely to collapse) should generally not execute reciprocal powers of attorney as a way of planning for incapacity. Should the breakup turn nasty, one partner who is legally entitled to act on the other's behalf might drain the other's savings account or squander his or her assets out of spite or greed. A **springing power of attorney** (page 103) is far safer.

Providing for Minor Children

If you die and your spouse survives you, he or she will naturally have custody of your minor children, so you might think there'll be no need for a personal guardian for them. Even if you're divorced, it's almost impossible for the custodial parent to deny the noncustodial parent custody of their child if the custodial parent should die. (There are rare exceptions, such as if the surviving parent is in jail or has been found incompetent by a court.)

If you leave all your estate to your spouse, the children will presumably have no property to manage, so you might think there'll also be no need for a guardian of their property.

But what if you both should die, perhaps in a car accident? Your will should provide for that real—if remote—possibility by nominating one or more persons to fill these roles.

If both parents die, the law requires a minor child to have a personal guardian to step in and, in effect, become the child's parent. Who would be the guardian for your children? Many people haven't given this question enough thought. Questions to consider:

- Who would provide the best care for your children if you die?

- Is the home you choose large enough for them?

- Will their guardians have enough money to provide your children with the kind of education and environment you prefer?

- What sort of financial provisions should you make for the children?

A will can nominate a personal guardian. In most cases, the probate judge doesn't have to accept the testator's choice—although unless someone challenges that choice as not being in the child's best interest, the court will almost always go along. In some states, a child of fourteen years or older may select his or her guardian.

It's better to nominate an individual as personal guardian; if you name a couple and they split up, what happens to the child? Be sure to consult with the person you name to be sure he or she wants the job, and name an alternative guardian in case your first choice should have a change of heart or die before the child is grown.

If you don't appoint a guardian for your children, someone

(usually a friend or relative) may ask the court to name him or her as guardian. If no one volunteers, the court can choose someone—generally, the nearest adult relative. Again, the guide is the child's best interest.

Property Guardians

What about the person who will look after the children's property—the property guardian or property manager? Children under eighteen can't legally own (without supervision) more than a minimal amount of property; the law requires an adult who is responsible for managing for the child's benefit all property above that minimal limit. You should definitely name a property guardian for your children, even if you don't leave them any money in your will, in case the other parent dies, too.

Who should be the property guardian? Generally, the same person you name to be the child's personal guardian. You can appoint two different people to manage the child's money and personal affairs, but be aware that conflicts may arise if you split authority this way. Still, if the personal guardian lacks the financial expertise or inclination to manage money, it may be worthwhile to consider another relative or friend to be the property guardian. Using a bank or other institution as a property manager may not be a wise idea, particularly for a small- to medium-sized estate; often, their fees are too high and they are too impersonal to provide the level of service you want and need.

The difficulty with property guardians is that the law usually requires the guardian to put up a bond, file all sorts of legal papers, account for finances, and negotiate a maze of legal requirements—all of which would be at least doubled if that guardian dies or resigns and a successor guardian is appointed.

For example, all but twelve states require that the property guardian post a bond, and in some of those states you can't waive the requirement in your will. There may also be restrictions on who may serve as the children's property guardian. That's why it's best to minimize the role of the property guardian by setting up a simple trust for your children in your will. The trust would probably be funded by life insurance policies on each parent's life, payable to the surviving spouse, or to the children's trust if both parents die simultaneously. It would go into effect at the death of the second parent.

In such a testamentary trust or a revocable trust to which property in the will pours over, you appoint someone (a trustee) to manage the assets you leave to your children, set forth the conditions under which money would be paid to them, and give the trustee authority to spend, sell, or invest the assets for the children's benefit. Typically, the trust would provide for the children's care and education and make money available to them as they reach certain ages indicative of maturity—eighteen, twenty-one, twenty-five, or thirty. Trusts are far more flexible than guardianships, which require court approval of actions by the guardian and usually must follow strict rules for paying out funds to children—rules that may not agree with your wishes as to which of your children should receive which of your assets and when.

Custodian Accounts

What if your estate is modest and you don't think it warrants setting up a trust for your children, but you still want to convey property to them upon your death? You can set up a custodian account for them while you are still alive and usually give funds to that account through your will. The Uniform Gifts to Minors Act (UGMA) or the Uniform Transfers to Minors Act (UTMA) have been adopted by almost all the states.

The UGMA and UTMA authorize the creation of custodian accounts for minors. Thus, they're different from bank accounts you'd open in a child's name. But the mechanism they authorize is so simple that you can probably set them up using just a bank or brokerage. These laws allow you to open an account in a child's name and deposit money or property in it while you are still alive. You can make yourself custodian of the account, and set up a successor in case you die while the child is under eighteen (or up to twenty-one or even twenty-five in some states). Use the child's Social Security number.

Both laws give the custodian broad powers, with the powers under the UTMA being somewhat wider. For example, an UGMA custodian cannot take title to real property unless the statute has been modified.

When your children are over age thirteen, the income in these accounts is taxed by the federal government at the children's rate, which will almost certainly be lower than yours. For younger children, through the "kiddie tax," the federal government taxes income from the account at *your* tax rate.

The drawbacks? Some parents might be uncomfortable with the fact that a child fourteen or older must pay taxes, or the fact that the money becomes the child's property when he or she reaches age eighteen, leaving you no control over it. Also, the kiddie tax doesn't give you any tax breaks. If you die before the child reaches eighteen, the funds revert to your estate and are taxed accordingly, unless you've named a third party as your successor custodian.

In the states that permit gifts by will to these accounts, you can also use this mechanism to leave a gift to children who aren't yours, such as a favorite nephew. Or you could set up a trust just as you would for your own children or leave it to the child's parents to be used for her benefit (although this wouldn't legally bind the parents to spend it on the child).

Using an UGMA, UTMA, or a trust will reduce the amount of supervision and paperwork required of a guardian by the court, and thus lower expenses to your estate. If most of the assets you leave to the child are handled by these methods, it can reduce the probate court's involvement to almost nothing. But even if you make gifts to your child in any of these ways, you still must name a personal guardian in your will, as well as a property guardian to manage property the child receives after you die and property inadvertently left out of the trust or UGMA/UTMA gift. You can make the same person the personal guardian, property guardian, custodian, and trustee.

Contingency Plans for Your Children

Of course, you want to provide for your children, but sometimes you don't get around to changing your will when you have a new child. The law helps you out in that case. If you've made a will, then have another child and die before you can change your will to include him or her, most states provide for a share of your property to go to this **pretermitted child**.

The share a pretermitted child is entitled to take varies from state to state. It also may depend on whether you left him or her a gift through some means other than a will (such as a living trust), and whether you had a surviving spouse or other children who received gifts in the will.

Generally, if you had no other children, the pretermitted child would receive the same share he or she would have received had you died intestate (without a will). If you had other children, yet gave them nothing under the will (often, people leave everything to the spouse), the pretermitted child would receive nothing, just like the other children. If, however, you left property to the other children, the omitted child may be entitled to what he or she would have received had you given each child an equal share. Thus, if you had two children and provided for them in the will, and a third was born later but left out of the will, the court would divide the amount of the estate you left to the other two children by three and give the pretermitted child one-third of the total.

If you want to avoid this result, the best way is to keep your will up-to-date and provide for these contingencies by specifically disinheriting any children you don't want to provide for. Obviously, if it could be shown that you had intentionally disinherited any children yet to be born—usually by language in the will—no pretermitted child laws apply. They also usually don't apply to nonprobate instruments like a living trust.

What happens if you will some of your property to one of your children but he or she dies before you do? Generally, a will can't make a gift to a dead person, so if a beneficiary dies before you, the gift lapses or fails (i.e., it goes back into your estate). However, most states have anti-lapse laws providing that a gift to a child or descendant who dies before you passes on to that person's descendants.

One way to accommodate late arrivals or early departures is not to bequeath your assets to children by name but as a class (e.g., "I leave all my property in equal shares to my children living at my death and to the then living descendants of each deceased child, the descendants of a deceased child to take their ancestor's share, *per stirpes*"). If you have three children when you make the will, and one dies before you do, the remaining two children will inherit one-half of your estate instead of one-third, unless the deceased child leaves descendants, in which event the descendants take the deceased child's share.

What about children who don't fit the traditional categories, such as adoptees, children from a previous marriage, or so-called illegitimate children? In most states, adopted children are treated just like natural children unless you indicate otherwise in your will. To avoid problems, specify in your will that "child," etc., includes (or excludes, as you wish) an adopted child. If your will simply indicates that gifts will go to your children (without indicating which), children from all your marriages will be included in that term. However, if you marry someone with children from a previous marriage and don't formally adopt these stepchildren as your own, they are not included in your bequest to your children unless you specifically say so. If you're a male, in most states a bequest to children includes only legitimate children and those who have proved paternity. But in the case of a mother, a bequest to children usually includes illegitimate ones as well.

Older Couples

Archie and Edith have paid off the mortgage on their home. They've accumulated many more assets than they had when they were young and have to be concerned about lowering the taxes on their estate. With retirement near, they're also concerned with assuring that the surviving spouse has enough funds for a comfortable life for his or her remaining years.

Like most older couples, they have left everything to the surviving spouse, with the expectation that the property will pass to the children or grandchildren upon his or her death.

Fred and Ethel, whose children have already established themselves well in the world, are less concerned about providing for their children and want instead to concentrate on leaving a gift (probably in trust) for their grandchildren, with the parents to administer it. Since the surviving spouse will likely not live many years beyond the other spouse, each has set up a **marital trust** effective upon his or her death. The surviving spouse would live off the income from the trust and at death the principal would go to the children or grandchildren.

Lucy and Ricky have enough assets to worry more about tax planning and giving gifts to friends and relatives outside their immediate family. To accomplish these goals, they created a **marital living trust**, which will avoid probate and help protect assets from taxes. They placed most of their assets in this living trust, and the surviving spouse receives the income from it for the rest of his or her life. When the second spouse dies, the property remaining in this life estate trust will pass on to their children or grandchildren. Other beneficiaries would receive gifts via a will, which also picks up assets not placed in the trust at the time of death. The successor trustee should be the child (and/or a professional trustee, if the estate is large enough) who is most capable of managing the money for the grandchildren's benefit. This type of vehicle requires the advice and active participation of a lawyer and other professional advisers.

Older couples, like younger, must plan for the possibility of their dying simultaneously. In that case, they'll want a provision that sets up a contingent gift for any grandchildren; that is, if one of your children dies before you do, the gift that would have gone to that child instead passes to his or her children when they reach age eighteen or twenty-one. Sometimes the gift will be structured so that a contingent trust comes into effect when you die, and the gift will be held in trust for the grandchildren till they reach majority age. Or the trustee can pay it out over time, so that the grandchildren don't suddenly have thousands of dollars at their disposal when they are still relatively young.

Bequests to Children

If you have more than one child, keep in mind that you don't have to leave money or property to your children in equal shares, although this is the most common arrangement. Rather, you can leave each child the kind and amount of assets that best suit his or her situation. The grown child who just graduated from medical school, for example, would probably need less of an inheritance from you than the learning disabled child who just turned nineteen. The son who shares your interest in ichthyology would probably appreciate your aquarium more than your daughter, the stock car racer.

Disinheriting Children

Children may be disinherited. In case your state has standards of specificity for disinheriting children, you should be sure to name in your will the children you intend to disinherit: "I intentionally make no provision for my son, Oedipus." In a few states, you must leave the disinherited children a token amount, usually a dollar, to make sure they don't get a share against your wishes. Louisiana, as usual, is an exception to the general rule. It has a "forced heirship" policy that, with certain exceptions, requires parents to leave a share of their estate to each of their children.

Childless Couples

Diana and Charles have no children. Each wants to leave his or her estate to the survivor of whoever dies first, but on the death of the survivor one-half is to go to designated relatives of Diana's and the other half to designated relatives of Charles's. To ensure this, they enter into a written agreement that provides that neither will make any change in his or her will so that on the death of the survivor the property will go in the manner specified in the contract. An executed copy is attached to each will. (See chapter 7.)

Single People

Married people aren't the only ones who need to plan their estates. If you're single and have children, you'll want to provide for guardianship using one of the techniques described above. (If you're cohabiting with a lover of the same or opposite sex, see chapter 7.) Whether or not you have children, you'll probably want to use a health-care power of attorney, living will, or other device discussed in chapter 12 to plan for your possible incapacity or terminal illness. You may want to pass certain property to certain people—your antique dresser to the niece who so admires it, your Cajun accordion to a music-loving friend—which you can do with your will (see chapter 3) or a living trust (see chapter 5). And if you're wealthy, you'll want to use tax-avoidance techniques (discussed briefly in chapter 8) to give your property to relatives, friends, or charities instead of the government. In short, as you read this book—whether you're thoroughly single, utterly married, or somewhere in between— look for estate-planning techniques that seem appropriate to your circumstances.

■

CHAPTER SEVEN

Special Considerations

M OST OF THIS BOOK deals with the "typical" estate-planning situation: a married couple of moderate
income with children. But increasingly, there is no typical American living arrangement. This chapter considers less common
situations that might require special arrangements in your will,
trust, or other parts of your estate plan.

Taking Against the Will

In a perfect world, all marriages would be blissful, but in reality
many aren't. Some spouses are shocked to learn that their partners, for whatever reason, wanted to cut them out of their wills.
However, the law usually doesn't permit this. In the days when
wives were totally dependent on their husbands, disinheritance
could leave widows destitute. Even though the law may have
originally been intended to protect widows, it applies both ways.
Women can't cut their husbands out of wills either.

If a husband or wife dies and his or her will makes no provision for the surviving spouse, or conveys to that person less than
a certain percentage of the deceased spouse's assets (the percentage varies by state), a surviving spouse can **take against the will**.
This means he or she can choose to accept the amount allowed
by law (usually a third or half of the estate) instead of the amount
bequeathed in the will. The surviving spouse doesn't have to
take against the will. If he or she chooses not to, the property is
bequeathed as stated in the will.

This **elective** or **forced share provision** is troubling to many people considering second marriages late in life. Many have avoided marriage out of fear that the surviving spouse of only a few years could take half their property, though they want to give it to their own children. Recent revisions to the Uniform Probate Code have adopted a sliding scale for widows or widowers who take against the will—that is, the longer the marriage, the higher the elective share. If the marriage lasted only a few years, the percentage could be quite low, minimizing one source of worry for older couples. Check with your lawyer to see if your state has adopted these revisions. Also, spouses in some states aren't entitled to a forced share of living trust assets—you can use living trusts in these jurisdictions to disinherit your spouse (see "Advantages of a Living Trust," chapter 5). Your lawyer can tell you whether these options are available in your state.

Prenuptial/Postnuptial Agreements

Another way to prevent a spouse from taking against the will is to execute an agreement in which the partners voluntarily give up the right to a statutory share of the other's estate and agree on how much—or how little—of the other's estate each will inherit. These agreements can be made before the marriage ceremony (prenuptial) or after it (postnuptial). They usually supersede statutory set-asides for spouses.

Actually, any couple in which one partner is substantially older or wealthier than the other should consider such an agreement. To ensure fairness, each one should be represented by a separate attorney when drawing up these agreements, and each should make a full disclosure of his or her assets. If this sounds anti-romantic or difficult to do—well, take another look at those divorce statistics.

Contract to Make a Will

What if the statutory share is too little? The statutory protection for spouses is often inadequate, especially if one spouse thinks he or she deserves certain items of property, such as the family home. Married couples in this situation might benefit from executing a **contract to make a will**, which guarantees how the property will be bequeathed (see below), or a prenuptial/postnuptial agreement.

SPLITTING UP: DIVORCE AND REMARRIAGE

Statistically, about half of all marriages now end in divorce, making this an important consideration in estate planning. Depending on the details of your state's law, divorce or annulment generally either revokes the entire will or those provisions in favor of the former spouse. In most states, however, that is not true of a revocable trust. The safest course is to revise your will and trust if you get divorced, changing the provisions that relate to your former spouse and his or her family, especially the residuary clause. The high divorce rate is another good reason for both partners to have separate wills.

Recent revisions of the Uniform Probate Code automatically revoke provisions of other estate documents, such as life insurance policies, in which the proceeds previously would have gone to the ex-spouse. But again, few states have adopted all provisions of the UPC; it's best to change any such documents, including living wills and survivorships, or have your lawyer do it. Trusts may need to be specifically amended, including names of trustees if they were members of your ex-spouse's family. Retirement benefits like pensions and IRAs will also have to be changed.

Couples who didn't execute a premarital agreement might consider a postmarriage agreement that accomplishes some of the same objectives: setting forth the division of property and the estate plan in the event the marriage dissolves.

The so-called **marital deduction** is one of the most important parts of estate tax planning, and when you divorce, you lose it. If your estate is worth more than $1 million, you will certainly need to revise your tax planning after a divorce.

Couples with Children from Different Marriages

If you're one member of a couple in which both you and your spouse have children from previous marriages, you might want to arrange things so your own money goes to your own children

DIFFERENT STATES, DIFFERENT FATES

There are sometimes big differences between the laws in different states, and if you own property in different states, or if you've moved since you planned your estate, you should check to be sure your estate plan conforms with applicable state law.

For example, what if you live in a separate property state but own real estate in a community property state? Often, state laws will treat such real estate as community property for estate-planning purposes. Thus, if you live in Arkansas (a separate property state) but own land in Texas, an Arkansas court probating your will would treat the Texas property just as Texas would—as community property. But not every state would extend the same courtesy.

Obviously, this separate/community property division can get pretty complicated—and it's only one example of how state laws are different. If you own property in more than one state, use a professional adviser who is conversant with the estate laws of all of them or consult an attorney in each state involved.

and your spouse's money goes to his or her children. If those children are well-off and earning their own incomes, then you might consider leaving more to your surviving spouse, or to other family members, perhaps by setting up a trust for your grandchildren, for example. Here is a brief discussion of some of the transfer techniques:

- **QTIP trusts—for heirs, not ears.** Providing for children from different marriages may conflict with tax planning. The marital deduction allows spouses to leave their entire estates to each other without paying taxes. What if you and your spouse have children (especially grown children) from other marriages? You might naturally prefer that your biological children receive more of your estate than your spouse's children from a previous marriage. If you leave your entire estate to your spouse, he or she might not agree—but has the final decision after you're gone.

That's why some "patchwork" families are using **Qualified**

Terminable Interest Property Trusts. The QTIP allows you to leave your property in trust for your spouse, but then it goes to whomever you wish after your spouse dies. You still get the marital deduction, your spouse gets to live off the income from the trust, and your children get the property upon their deaths. The problem: no one else can benefit from the assets in the trust until your spouse dies, which might not leave other family members enough money for their comfort until then. Insurance can ease the blow. If you have a large enough estate, you can leave up to $1 million (tax-free under current law) to your children or in a trust for their benefit upon your death and put the rest into the QTIP trust.

• **Mutual wills.** Mutual wills provide another option where children from different marriages (or anyone else that you want to inherit some of your property) are involved. Each spouse agrees to leave all property to the survivor, who after death will leave specified property to the friends or relatives the other designates. Warning: Use of mutual wills might jeopardize the marital tax deduction and also involves issues of contract law that vary among states. Get professional advice before using this strategy.

Don't confuse **mutual wills** (two separate wills that refer to each other and are trying to accomplish the same purpose) with a **joint and mutual will** (one will that attempts, usually unsuccessfully, to cover two people). See page 36.

• **Life estates.** What if you want your surviving spouse to be able to live in the family home but also want to make sure that it will ultimately pass to your children? A life estate is an option. A **life estate** means that the recipient only gets to use the property for as long as he or she lives, then it is passed to a third party (or occasionally reverts to your estate). It can't be sold or substantially modified by the life tenant. Your will can include this provision, but check with a lawyer before trying such property conveyances—they can be quite complex. A better method is to leave it in trust for your spouse so long as he or she is able and wants to occupy it. Be sure to spell out what obligations the occupant assumes.

- **Life insurance.** Life insurance is another tool you can use to distribute assets among children from different marriages. You can set up an irrevocable trust for your children that's funded from the proceeds of a life insurance policy. You pay the premiums, but the trust actually owns the policy. When you die, your children receive the benefits from the trust while your spouse gets the rest of your estate. Such a device is often helpful in providing funds for payment of estate taxes on the death of the surviving husband or wife.

- **Trusts.** The versatility of trusts makes them useful instruments for allocating assets among different families because you can set up a separate trust for the children of different marriages or even for each family member.

- **Prenuptial and postnuptial agreements.** If you're an older person with grown children from another marriage, you should strongly consider asking your lawyer, as part of your estate plan, to prepare a pre- or postnuptial agreement that specifies that the separate property of each spouse remains separate at death. Then, your wills or will substitutes can leave your assets directly to your respective children on your death. They're already adults, and it's unlikely your spouse will survive you long enough to require large amounts of money from your estate to live on.

- **Contract to make a will or not revoke a will.** Such a contract prevents your spouse from changing arrangements in his or her will without your knowledge and consent. These can supersede any updated will and can be written so that they expire if the marriage officially ends in divorce or annulment. In effect, such a contract guarantees that each person will stick to the jointly agreed-upon estate plan, instead of changing a will without the other's knowledge. The obvious drawback is that since a contract cannot be changed without the other person's permission no matter how much your circumstances change, it surrenders the flexibility that a will provides. These contracts are usually prepared in anticipation that some conflict will occur; therefore, each party should be represented by his or her lawyer.

One thing to keep in mind: Patchwork families are a prime category for will contests, as children from different marriages may be more likely to disagree about the distribution of estate assets. People in this category should be especially careful that their wills, pre-/postnuptial agreements, or contracts to make a will, are properly prepared.

- **Joint tenancy.** If your combined estate falls under the $1 million limit, and you don't expect it to exceed that amount by the time the second spouse dies, it's sometimes simpler just to leave all the property in joint tenancy because then the surviving spouse receives all the assets without worrying about estate tax and there's no probate. However, you still need to take into account the drawbacks of joint tenancy discussed in chapter 2, especially the fear that the surviving spouse will squander the money instead of spending it on the children or will remarry and leave all the money to the new family. Since joint tenancy doesn't let you control the distribution of your money after you die, you will have to put the property in another form of ownership if you want it to go to anyone but your spouse.

UNMARRIED PARTNERS

The law is almost always written with conventional families in mind. That's why it has provisions like the **spouse's elective share** and the **rules of intestacy**, which leave your property to your family if you die without a will. For unmarried couples to do all that married couples can do in the eyes of the law, each partner must have a will or trust and use contractual agreements that set out each partner's rights and responsibilities.

If you're an unmarried couple, you'll probably have many of the same estate-planning objectives as married couples. For example, each of you will probably want to provide immediate help for your partner if you die, possibly through life insurance. Depending on what assets you have, you may want a revocable trust with a pourover will just like a married couple would have.

You'll have to figure out what will happen to your bank account, to your partner's bank account, to a joint bank account, and other property should one of you die. It's especially important to make provisions for property acquired while you and your partner have been living together. The real problems in cases like these are often expensive items of personal property: collectibles, art collections, furniture, and so on.

Consider the following options for unmarried partners:

• **Wills.** It's especially important for unmarried partners to have wills because state intestacy laws presume that your blood relatives will inherit your property after you die when, in fact, you may want your property to go to your partner.

• **Cohabitation agreements.** Cohabitation agreements, which can cover a wide range of topics, are also worth considering.

To deal with each partner's possible disability, for example, **cohabitation agreements** often contain **mutual powers of attorney** that enable partners to act on each other's behalf. However, you'd better be careful. **Durable powers of attorney**, which are usually used for business transactions, enable the other person to spend your money, sign your name to binding documents, and so on. Many unmarried people might want their partners to have this kind of authority if they should become disabled by age, injury, or disease but not when they are in full possession of their faculties. If you don't want your partner to have all this power (and you may not if the relationship is tenuous), have your lawyer write the power of attorney so it is **springing**; that is, it takes effect only when you have been certified incompetent by your physician. But make sure your state's law allows this.

Another option is to execute a **health-care power of attorney** that allows your "significant other" to make medical decisions if you should become incapacitated but doesn't give him or her control over your bank account and other nonmedical affairs.

• **Guardianships or conservatorships.** A cohabitation agreement might also provide for **mutual guardianships**, so that if one partner becomes disabled, the other can take care of him or her. This is especially important if one partner's family doesn't accept the validity of your alternative lifestyle; should you become disabled without prior legal arrangements, the courts can appoint a guardian and will often lean toward a family member over someone with no legal status.

• **Contract to make a will.** Anyone can change a will at any time. But each partner in a married couple is somewhat protected against sudden, capricious changes of mind by state laws that allow a spouse to take against the will. The law doesn't extend this sort of protection to unmarried partners.

Suppose you're putting your partner through medical school and you stand to inherit a lot of her property. After making such a sacrifice, you don't want her to change her mind without your knowing about it and rewrite her will leaving her property to someone else.

To prevent this, you might as part of your cohabitation agreement execute a contract to make a will, which legally binds both of you to its terms. The contract can only be changed by attacking it in court, a much more difficult procedure than rewriting a will. Usually these contracts contain a provision that dissolves them when the partners agree in writing that the relationship is over. They might also provide that the wills of both parties be kept at the lawyer's office and that neither can obtain access to them without the other being present. Obviously, these documents should be custom-tailored to the particular concerns and circumstances of each relationship and probably will require a lawyer to do them right.

• **Trusts.** Unmarried couples with sufficient assets and a cohabitation agreement might find living trusts useful, if they can stand the inconvenience of keeping track of which property goes into which trust. Each partner might set up a separate living trust for his or her separate property and possibly a third one together for shared property. The individual trusts can be used to make gifts for friends or relatives of each partner; the shared

FINE, FEATHERED, OR FURRY FRIENDS

Every pet owner knows that pets are part of the family—in the hearts of their owners if not in the eyes of the law. Law books are full of wills that tried to provide for pets people left behind. Especially in recent years, these provisions are almost always thrown out. You generally can't leave money or property directly to an animal nor can you make it the direct beneficiary of a trust.

The one way to provide in a will for a pet's care is to make an agreement with someone to take care of it after you die and bequeath an amount of money needed to pay for the care to that person. You also need to provide for what happens to that money after the pet dies.

A trust is usually a better way to provide for your pets; leave the animal and some money for its care in trust to a friend who is named beneficiary.

trust can leave property to the couple's mutual friends as well as to the surviving partner.

A final word: The law frequently revokes wills (and sometimes other documents) when a couple's marriage ends. It doesn't provide such a fail-safe for the wills of nonmarried partners, their cohabitation agreements, contracts to make a will, etc. You can write into the cohabitation agreement or contract a provision that alters the will and other documents if the parties agree that the relationship is over. If you don't, you must remember to deal with these documents should the relationship dissolve.

In any event, you should certainly rewrite your estate plan when this happens, as with any major life change.

GAY AND LESBIAN COUPLES

Most of the information in the preceding section applies to gay and lesbian couples as well as to unmarried heterosexual partners. Since gay and lesbian couples face legal barriers that heterosexuals don't, estate planning is even more critical for them.

When it comes to relationships, the law is basically written for people who are married. You may recall the Sharon Kowalski case, in which the courts gave custody of a nearly comatose young woman to her family despite evidence that she would have preferred that important decisions be made by her lesbian partner. Had she been married, a court would probably have given custody to her husband.

You can't count on the law or a judge to be sympathetic to gay and lesbian relationships. If you are gay and in a relationship with someone whom you want to include in your estate plan, you have to take extra steps to prevent family members (some of whom might not approve of homosexual relationships) from interfering with your wishes.

Much of what heterosexual partners take for granted—the ability to take out family life insurance policies, file joint tax returns, inherit pension benefits, or make medical decisions for each other in the event of disability—will not automatically apply to homosexual relationships. You have to take additional, affirmative steps to protect your rights and make certain you have an estate plan that meets your needs. While some people dislike bringing prosaic legal concerns into a romantic relationship, think of these procedures as legal recognition of your commitment to the relationship, the same as marriage is for heterosexuals.

Consider the following:

• **Wills.** It's especially important to write a will if you're involved in a same-sex relationship because it lets you leave your property to anyone or any organization you wish, even though the law may not officially recognize your relationship. Most important, a will lets you name an executor for your estate to supervise distribution of your assets. If, as is likely, you want your partner to inherit a good share of your property, naming your partner or someone sympathetic to the relationship as executor will help ensure that your wishes are carried out.

• **Beneficiary designations.** As important as it is to write a will, remember that that's not enough to assure that all your property goes to your partner. As discussed in chapter 2, many assets pass by means other than a will. So if you want your partner to receive the proceeds from a life insurance policy, IRA, bank account, and so on, you need to name your partner as the beneficiary in each of those documents separately.

The advantage of using beneficiary designations and other nonprobate arrangements (such as holding property in joint tenancy with your partner) is that the transfers take place automatically on your death; no disgruntled relative can hold up your wishes as they can in a will contest.

• **Funeral instructions.** Funeral instructions can be an especially important subject for homosexual couples. Since the law often gives the deceased person's blood relatives—not the same-sex partner—the right to determine what will be said at the funeral, what will appear in a newspaper notice, and so on, many surviving partners have been disappointed to find that no mention has been made of the relationship or even the fact that the deceased was gay. To prevent this, write up a list of funeral instructions as indicated in chapter 11, naming your partner (if that's who you want) as the person responsible for carrying out those instructions. You might mention the instructions in your will as well, although you should remember that sometimes a funeral is over before the will is read. Still, the mention of your wishes in a will and a signed statement of funeral instructions should go a long way toward convincing funeral directors of your partner's authority in the event of a dispute.

• **Powers of attorney.** A durable power of attorney gives your partner, or anyone else you choose, the legal authority to handle your financial affairs, pay the bills, deposit and withdraw money from the bank, and so on if you become incompetent. A health-care durable power of attorney lets you decide who has the right to make medical decisions for you should you become incapacitated (see chapter 12).

For all these arrangements, especially cohabitation agreements, you should seek out a lawyer who's experienced in nonspousal domestic partnerships. Your local gay rights organization may keep a listing of attorneys who specialize in such situations.

See chapter 12 for information on estate planning for people with AIDS.

BUSINESS OWNERS

Small business owners have a host of special needs. Who will take over the business upon your disability or after you die? Which child gets control of the stock? Which one runs the company, and which merely share in the profits?

The principal issues your estate plan should address are:

• Who will run the business if you're disabled? Do you want the business to continue after your death? If so, who will run it?

• What's the best way to transfer ownership to the new owners?

• Will your beneficiaries be capable of taking over the business—and will they even want to?

Before you meet with your lawyer to plan your estate (and the legal issues involved here are so touchy that a lawyer's expertise is essential), you should sit down with your beneficiaries and business partners and answer these critical questions.

If your beneficiaries (usually we're talking about a spouse and children) are interested in taking over the business and in your judgment possess the expertise to do so, it's relatively simple to transfer your interest directly to them. If stock is involved, you might want to leave voting stock to the children who will be involved in operating the business and nonvoting stock to the others. Or you can leave the child who will be running the business enough cash (perhaps through life insurance proceeds) to enable him or her to buy out the rest of the estate and thus avoid conflicts.

Sometimes your beneficiaries will want no part of the business after you're gone. Things get slightly more complicated if you decide to pass management or ownership to people who are not beneficiaries of your will. If so, and if your business is a partnership, you'll usually want the other partners to remain in operational control of the company. The most common device used for transferring ownership of a business on the death of a partner is the **buy-sell agreement**, in which all the remaining partners agree to purchase the interest of any partner who dies. This allows the business to continue running smoothly with the same people in charge, minus one.

Buy-sell agreements typically provide that at the owner's death, his or her interest in the business will be acquired by the remaining partners or shareholders, leaving the dead partner's relatives with the proceeds of the sale. Life insurance is usually the vehicle used to finance these arrangements, which lets the business itself avoid a drain on its cash. The partners buy life insurance on each other's lives and the proceeds go to the surviving spouses, children, or whomever in return for the deceased partner's share of the business.

There are two principal ways to structure such agreements. An **entity purchase** allows the business itself to take out a policy on the life of each owner and use the proceeds to purchase the share of a deceased owner. With a **cross-purchase**, the co-owners each take out insurance on each other and each buys a share of the dead partner's interest. While an entity purchase is simpler, a cross-purchase may provide a substantial tax advantage.

Avoiding probate can be more important than usual where a business is concerned, since even relatively short interruptions in transferring title to bank accounts and other assets through probate can be devastating to a business that must pay its bills on time. The people who take over from you might find they have to get probate court approval for major business decisions for up to three months unless you have made adequate arrangements to avoid this. So you might do well to arrange for the business assets to pass outside your will, usually through a trust or contractual agreement.

The estate tax rules for small businesses differ from those covering individuals, so you'll need to consult a lawyer or certified financial planner, chartered financial consultant, or other professional with experience in this difficult area of law and finance.

DEBTORS AND CREDITORS

Most estate planning assumes that you have assets to distribute when you die. But what if you're in debt, and even after the life insurance pays off beneficiaries there's only red ink in your estate account?

First, don't fear that your family will "inherit" your debts through your will. Only if they co-signed on notes or otherwise made some contractual agreement to assume liability for debts can any of your beneficiaries be stuck with any of your debts. If you should will someone an asset that's burdened by debt (e.g., a house or business), the recipient may **disclaim** the gift and therefore not receive it—or the debt attached to it.

By law, estate debts must be paid before assets are distributed. So if your spouse left credit card debts, for example, and you hadn't co-signed the card agreement the company couldn't pursue you to pay her debts (except in a community property state) but it would be entitled to take its share out of the estate before you received your inheritance.

If your estate's debts exceed the assets, they must be satisfied in a particular order set by your state's law. The executor of a debt-ridden estate will, under the court's supervision, pay off the debts in the prescribed order.

If the debts do not exceed the assets, then after the executor pays them the remaining assets can be distributed. The process of liquidating assets to pay debts might provide some of your beneficiaries with a windfall, others with a shortfall. If you gave your Texas bank accounts to your spouse and your Alaska accounts to your brother, for example, and the Texas bank accounts were scoured first to pay the debts, your spouse might be left holding the (empty) bag as your brother drives away into the sunset.

This hardly seems fair, and to prevent such a problem, you can provide that all gifts in your will be proportionately reduced so that after the debts are paid off each beneficiary's gift is reduced by the same percentage. So if after paying all debts your estate contains only 50 percent of the money that you direct be distributed through the will, each recipient's gift would be cut in half.

If your estate is forced into bankruptcy when you die, it will be managed by a trustee just as any other bankrupt concern would be. Creditors get in line to collect according to the bankruptcy law's priorities.

CHAPTER EIGHT

■

Death and Taxes

EVER SINCE Caesar Augustus imposed an estate levy to pay for imperial Roman exploits, death and taxes have walked hand in bony hand. Today, they're even more closely linked; as cash-strapped governments cast about for new sources of revenue, they're likely to at least look at raising estate taxes.

This chapter discusses some of the issues everyone, no matter how wealthy, ought to know about death and taxes. Going beyond that presents a dilemma here. Tax planning is the core of much estate law, but it is important to people with substantial assets—at least $800,000—which might appreciate to at least $1 million, the estate tax threshold in 2002 and 2003. (This threshold will rise gradually; see below.) Even if you aren't rich now and don't expect to be, this chapter provides a very brief discussion of the basic tax-reduction methods for estates. Then, if your estate grows or the law changes, you'll know what to talk to your lawyer about.

The Federal Estate Tax: General Principles

Your estate isn't liable for federal estate taxation unless it exceeds the available exemption amount. This is the value of assets that each person may pass on to beneficiaries without paying federal estate tax. The Economic Growth and Tax Relief Reconciliation Act of 2001 provides for a gradual increase in the exemption. Prior to the act, it was $675,000; in 2002 and 2003 it is $1 million; it will go up in increments, to $3.5 million in 2009, though most of the increase takes place in the last year. (See the chart on page 125.) In addition, you can pass your entire estate without any estate taxes to your spouse. (This is referred to as the **unlimited marital deduction**.) If you simply leave your estate to your spouse and don't create an appropriate trust to take advantage of your exemption, your spouse's estate will pay taxes on this sum when he or she dies.

To decide what the property in your estate is worth, the IRS does not look at what you paid for it but generally uses the fair market value of property you own at your death—or, if there is a tax that is payable by reason of your death and the total value six months from date of death is lower, your executor may elect to use that alternate valuation. In many cases—especially if you've owned your home for many years—the appreciation in value of large assets could put you over the limit. For appraisal purposes, the government uses the face value of insurance policies in your name, including most group policies from work or professional organizations, but only the cash value on someone else's life if you die before it has matured.

To the extent your estate exceeds the available exemption, the federal estate tax rates start at 37 percent. The assets subject to tax at death may include the family home, the family farm, life insurance, household furnishings, benefits under employee benefit plans, and other items that produce no lifetime income. In short, you may be richer than you think. If your estate is likely to exceed the threshold, however, good estate planning can sharply reduce the amount of money that goes to the government instead of to your beneficiaries.

Although the federal estate tax misses most people, it hits the rest hard: It is at least 37 percent and may be as high as 50 percent. So if you are in jeopardy of exceeding the threshold, be sure to perform an asset inventory (see appendix) and then see your lawyer if you need further tax planning.

Tax laws frequently change. Unfortunately, most people do not review their estate plans regularly. In light of the 2001 Act, you must check your estate planning documents to ensure that they still effectively shelter your estate tax exemption. If your will or living trust specifies a dollar amount, it will have to be revised. Have other specific aspects of your plan reviewed to assure that it is still effective.

JOINTLY OWNED PROPERTY AND THE FEDERAL ESTATE TAX

*In valuing jointly owned property, the IRS generally divides all **joint tenancy** property held by spouses equally between them, no matter who paid for it, so your estate will be credited with half the value of the family home, even if your spouse paid for the whole thing. (In the nine community property states, married couples hold most property as community property, so each has a half interest.)*

If you are well-off, holding all of your property in joint tenancy with your spouse may waste one of the two $1 million federal estate tax exemptions each couple holds in 2002 and 2003 (see above).

Furthermore, in most cases property you own in joint tenancy with right of survivorship with someone other than your spouse may be taxed on the basis of its total value, not just your share of it. For example, if you co-own a $90,000 house with your sister, all $90,000 may be considered part of your estate when you die unless your executor can demonstrate that your sister paid a portion of the purchase price and any improvements. For this reason, many lawyers urge clients to avoid owning too much property in joint tenancy.

*If you co-own property as a **tenant in common**, in contrast, your estate is only liable for tax on the percentage of ownership you had in the property: If you owned 25 percent of a $100,000 house, the government would add $25,000 to the value of your estate.*

*There is a way to convert jointly held property into two trusts that can combine many of the benefits of joint tenancy with the tax advantages of a trust. **Joint tenancy undisclosed trustee titleholding**, as it is known, is too complex to go into here but you might ask your lawyer about it, especially if you have a large estate.*

State Taxes on Estates and Inheritances

The federal estate tax rules apply to everyone in America. If you live in one of the states not listed in this paragraph or the District of Columbia, your worries end there. But you should know that there are state **death taxes**. Ohio charges an additional estate tax similar to the national one, and Connecticut, Indiana, Iowa, Kentucky, Louisiana, Maryland, Michigan, Nebraska, New Hampshire, New Jersey, North Carolina, Oklahoma, Pennsylvania, and Tennessee impose an inheritance tax. (**Inheritance taxes** are charged to beneficiaries, **estate taxes** to a person's estate.) Six states impose a separate gift tax, on top of the federal gift tax. (**Gift taxes** are imposed upon gifts made above a certain amount; see below.) What's taxed and at what rate depends on the law of the state you live in for intangible personal property, whenever located, and of the state in which it is located for real estate and tangible personal property. Some states, like Illinois and Florida, have only a "pick-up" tax, which is equal to the maximum credit the Internal Revenue Code allows to the taxpayer for state inheritance taxes. More states might impose death taxes as the federal tax is phased out.

Unless your state has an inheritance tax, your beneficiaries don't pay tax when they receive money from your estate. But they will have to pay income tax on any earnings after they invest the bequest.

Capital Gains Taxes

Death itself produces a large amount of extraordinary expenditures for taxes, expenses of administering the estate, and frequently the forced early payment of outstanding debts. To obtain the cash for such payments, sales of assets are frequently made, and if the sale is for more than the date-of-death value, it may trigger a capital gains tax at the time of sale. The asset selected for sale is critical, as the tax may be deferred or accelerated depending on present or future anticipated tax brackets.

Employee Benefits

Payments under company-deferred compensation and pension plans produce a bewildering array of possible choices (lump sum, installments, etc.), with differing income and estate tax results. The federal estate tax may not apply to some employer-provided annuities or death benefits paid to your beneficiaries. Social Security payments to your dependents are not subject to federal estate tax.

Proceeds from pensions and benefit plans generally pass

directly to whomever is named as a beneficiary in those plans. If, however, the proceeds are payable to the deceased's estate, they are part of the gross estate for estate tax purposes. Ask your lawyer or accountant about the possible tax consequences of your particular plan.

Taxes on Insurance Benefits

Many states impose an inheritance or estate tax on insurance proceeds payable to the estate. Some may also do so if insurance proceeds are payable to a named beneficiary, including the trustee of either a living trust or a trust created by a will, as long as the decedent owned this policy or held incidents of ownership (see below). However, the proceeds of an insurance policy paid to a named beneficiary are exempt from all federal income taxes, and almost all state income taxes except to the extent that they include interest.

You can save on estate taxes by transferring ownership of your life insurance policy to a trust that meets certain require-ments. This means the value of the proceeds won't be included in your estate. However, you must follow strict requirements:

- The life insurance trust must be irrevocable (see chapter 4).

- You cannot retain any kind of ownership (**incidents of ownership**), such as making decisions about the policy, or name yourself trustee.

- You must transfer the ownership at least three years before you die; otherwise, the proceeds will be taxed as part of your estate. The three-year rule doesn't apply if you were never the owner of the policy; for example, you could originally take out the policy in the name of the trust or of your spouse.

Income Tax Planning

An estate and a trust each constitute a separate taxpayer for in-come tax purposes (with exceptions for living trusts—see chapter 5), and this offers a broad range of tax-planning options. For example, the timing of paying estate expenses and making distributions have critical tax implications. Moreover, there are income tax options for series E and H savings bonds, the filing of a joint return with the surviving spouse, the deduction of medical expenses, and highly sophisticated techniques for timing of distributions to beneficiaries.

Expenses of administration may be used as either an income tax deduction on taxes owed by the estate or estate tax deduction (but not both). In the last year of the estate, such expenses can even be handled so as to be deductible directly or indirectly from the tax return of the individual beneficiaries.

This means that your survivors may have to make some tough calls about how and when to take certain deductions or make certain tax payments after you die. It's a good idea to plan ahead for competent financial and legal advice.

Selection of a legal and tax adviser after death is only half the battle, though, for no adviser can help if the family member in charge (whether an executor, surviving spouse, trustee, etc.) lacks the powers and discretion to make the proper tax choices. Most states give the necessary authority by statute, unless the person making the will provides otherwise, but none covers all possible conflict-of-interest questions. Furthermore, no state statutes cover the need for specific will clauses governing distribution of family home, car, furnishings, and the like. If you don't put such information in your will or trust, your beneficiaries may suffer unexpected income tax consequences after your estate assets are eventually distributed.

If you don't specify otherwise in your will, many states that have a death tax force the executor of your will to charge each person who receives anything from your estate a portion of the taxes on the estate. Other states provide that death taxes will be taken out of the residue of your estate.

Tax Planning if You Know You're Dying

This may sound morbid, but if you know you're going to die soon, you may be able to give more to your survivors by manipulating your income today. For example, you might choose to take

REFUSING BEQUESTS

Don't laugh—to reduce taxes or for other reasons, sometimes your beneficiaries may not want their bequests. For example, if you go bankrupt and then your father dies, your creditors may be entitled to first shot at the assets he leaves to you. You might want to give up the gift so that it will go to your children instead of your creditors. Or you may receive property that's subject to liens and mortgages greater than its market value.

*Most states permit you to **disclaim** (i.e., renounce or refuse) the inheritance or benefit. The Internal Revenue Code describes how a beneficiary may disclaim an interest in an estate for estate tax purposes. State law also defines how to disclaim for purposes of state death taxes; usually the two standards are the same. The beneficiary typically has to disclaim all the gift and must do so within nine months of becoming eligible for it.*

Once you disclaim a gift, the law generally acts as if you died before the testator so far as the gift is concerned. If the will or trust provides that should you die before the decedent, your share will go to your children, the children will take it if you disclaim the gift. You should see a lawyer if you intend to disclaim any gift.

capital losses while you're still alive, which, because of tax law treatment at death, can save your survivors money at tax time.

You can also make your annual, tax-deductible IRA contribution sooner than usual and give charities the gifts you'd planned to leave in your will, removing those assets from your estate and also giving you an income tax deduction, which won't matter to you after you're gone but will leave more money in the estate for your beneficiaries. (You can make such gifts even if you're incapacitated as long as you had the foresight to include such giving powers under a power of attorney.) If you do make such gifts, ask the recipient to give you a receipt, as required under a 1993 law for any gift of $250 or more to charity. This will help your executor show that the gift satisfies the bequest that was going to be made in the will (if that was your intention); it will avoid confusion at probate time.

You could also make charitable gifts in your will. These, too, would reduce the value of your estate and so reduce taxes.

Of course, if you're able, you'll also want to consider quickly implementing some of the other tax saving devices mentioned in this chapter, like interspousal transfers and annual tax-free gifts. But consider doing all this planning *now*, instead of on your deathbed, when you'll have other, more eternal concerns to occupy you.

TAX PLANNING FOR LARGER ESTATES

As your assets approach the available exemption amount, you need to consider a number of tax issues in your estate planning over and above those discussed earlier in this chapter. You assuredly need a lawyer's help in this complex matter; here we very briefly discuss a few options.

Any estate whose gross, not net, assets exceed the available exemption amount must file an estate tax return, even if deductions and other tax-avoidance methods mean the estate ultimately owes no tax. If the estate does owe a tax, and nothing in the will specifies which assets will be used to pay it, state law will usually charge the taxes to the beneficiaries on a proportional basis. In other words, the more you inherit from an estate, the more of the estate tax you have to pay out of the assets you inherit. Or state law may take taxes first from the residuary estate. Most people, however, specify in their wills certain funds to be used specifically to pay taxes; the tax is due in cash nine months from the date of death.

On the other hand, no asset received from a deceased individual is subject to income taxes on receipt. Once received, however, all income generated by that asset is subject to income tax on the tax return of the beneficiary. So your daughter who inherited your MTV stock wouldn't pay tax on the gift itself, but would pay tax on any income earned.

• **Bypass trusts.** The best way to minimize estate taxes is to use trusts. One of the most common of these is the **bypass trust** or **credit shelter trust**, also called the **exemption trust**. This trust is one of the primary estate-planning tools. It employs one of the main provisions of federal estate tax law, the **unified credit**, which currently gives each person a $1 million total exemption from estate and gift taxation ($3.5 million in 2009; see chart). It's called a bypass trust because the available exemption bypasses the surviving spouse's taxable estate and goes directly to a trust that ultimately benefits the children, grandchildren, or other beneficiaries when the second spouse dies.

Here is how it works. Assume that Jason dies and is survived by his wife, Medea, and several children. The adjusted gross estate (his estate after deducting funeral expenses, expenses of administration, and claims) totals $2 million. His will (or trust) creates a gift of $1 million for his wife (or a gift in trust; see below). The remaining $1 million goes into a family trust. The income of the trust is payable to Medea for as long as she lives. Medea also is entitled to the principal of the trust under an ascertainable standard of living, and she can have special power of appointment and act as trustee. On her death, her estate and the trust go to the children.

This arrangement minimizes or eliminates federal estate taxes. On Jason's death, his estate owes no estate tax. Because unlimited property can be passed to a spouse without being taxed (see below), the gift to Medea is exempt from federal estate taxes when Jason dies. It is added to Medea's taxable estate, but then her available exemption kicks in, so no taxes will be owed on her death if her taxable estate is not larger than the available exemption amount. The family trust utilizes her husband's exemption as a credit shelter trust on his death, but is not included in Medea's adjusted gross estate on her death.

• **Spousal trusts.** If you and your spouse's combined estate exceeds $2 million in 2002 and 2003, a bypass trust alone won't be enough to avoid the estate tax. In such cases, you have several options. But most attorneys would probably recommend that you next use a **spousal** or **marital deduction trust** (in addition to the bypass trust) to help you take full advantage of the second major estate tax planning device, the marital deduction. Spousal trusts are only available to married couples.

One of the most basic tax-planning devices is the unlimited **marital deduction**. It allows one spouse to pass his or her entire estate, regardless of size, to the other—and not pay federal estate taxes. No matter how large the estate, no taxes are due where it is passed to the spouse. If you only cared about leaving your property to your spouse, that would end your tax worries. Most people, however, want to leave property to their families at the death of the second spouse—and this is where tax planning pays off. Special rules apply to qualify for the marital deduction if the spouse is not a U.S. citizen.

Using the marital deduction properly, usually in conjunction with a tax-saving trust (as explained below), you should be able to transfer at least $2 million (in 2002 and 2003) free of estate taxes to your children or other beneficiaries no matter which spouse dies first or who accumulated the wealth.

There are two commonly used spousal trusts.

- **Power of appointment trust.** This is structured so that one spouse gives a trustee property to be held for the benefit of the other spouse, providing the other spouse with the use of the principal and all the income. Either during the donor's life or at his death, his spouse receives a **general power of appointment** that permits her to determine where the property should go after her death—to the children, charity, other beneficiaries, etc. Like all trusts, it avoids probate. It will generally qualify for the marital deduction and thus escape taxation at the death of the first spouse. The only major problem with a power of appointment trust is that it gives your surviving spouse total discretion over what happens to your money after you die.

- **QTIP trusts.** People who are afraid of giving up so much control to the spouse often turn to the second principal spousal trust. A **qualified terminable interest property—QTIP—trust** is a spousal trust that doesn't grant the spouse a power of appointment. It's especially good for people who want to make sure their children aren't slighted if their surviving spouse remarries or has his or her own children or other beneficiaries whom he or she prefers.

There are many other tax-saving trusts, among them **generation-skipping trusts**. Trusts generally benefit your children, but you can keep saving taxes and provide for your descendants for several generations after your death using a generation-skipping trust. Such a trust is quite versatile, allowing your family to use the money for college costs, medical expenses, large purchases such as homes, and general support. And it avoids or limits estate taxes on the estates of your children. It is too complicated to explain fully here, but generally in a generation-skipping trust instead of distributing all the money in the trust to your children on your death you leave as much as $1 million to future generations. This way, you can keep your assets out of the hands of children who might squander it or lose it in a divorce. If you put more than $1 million in a generation-skipping trust, it is subject to generation-skipping taxation, but if you put in less than $1 million it can grow beyond that amount through investments and interest. Generally, you use more than one trustee: an adult child and a lawyer or trust company to provide continuity.

Giving It Away—While You're Still Alive

Trusts are the devices of choice for minimizing taxes on estates of up to $1.35 million. The most common way to avoid taxes on estates larger than this is to use lifetime gifts. The law allows you to give up to $10,000 worth of assets *per recipient* to as many people as you wish each year (married donors giving a gift as a couple are allowed a $20,000 per recipient per year gift tax exclusion). This is called an **annual exclusion** in IRS-speak. You can also make tax-free, direct payments of tuition and medical expenses beyond the $10,000 limit. There is no gift tax on any gifts made between spouses in any amount nor on gifts to charitable organizations. You can use such lifetime gifts to reduce your estate to the tax-exempt level.

• **The gift tax marital deduction.** Similar to the estate tax marital deduction, this lets spouses (who are both U.S. residents) transfer an unlimited amount of money to each other at any time without gift tax concerns of any kind. Your lawyer can use these tax-free gifts to shift ownership of property between you and your spouse so that each spouse may make full use of his or her unified credit.

• **Gift giving with trusts.** The drawback to lifetime gifts is that you lose control of the money. Even assuming you leave yourself enough to live on comfortably, the beneficiary (usually a child) may not be responsible enough to handle that kind of money wisely. There are a couple of options to avoid this total loss of control. The first is to use life insurance (see below). The second is to give the money via a trust.

• **Charitable gifts.** Any gift to an approved charity you make during your lifetime, or bequeath at your death, is exempt from federal (and almost all state) gift and estate taxes. And the value of any bequests to charity is subtracted from the value of your estate when the federal estate tax is computed, meaning you can reduce those taxes by giving gifts to charity. There are many ways to help a good cause and help yourself at the same time. You can give stock that has appreciated in value over the years to a charity, and that way your estate won't have to pay the taxes on the increased value of the stock.

• **Split gifts.** A split gift is typically one where the grantor has retained some interest either for himself or for his beneficiaries and given the other interest away either to his beneficiaries or charity. Be aware, though, that such gifts may be taxed to your estate because you have retained an interest. Consult your lawyer.

• **Charitable remainder trust.** This mechanism is typically used by older people whose estates exceed $1 million and include appreciated assets, such as real estate or securities. You donate the asset to the trust, live off the income from the asset for the rest of your life, and then the trust principal goes to the charity you choose on your death (or on the death of your spouse if it's set up in both your names and he or she dies last). You avoid estate taxes and capital gains taxes while at the same time helping a charitable cause.

Remember also that taxes aren't the only factor in estate planning. Be careful not to give away too much money or too many assets that you might need for emergencies, living expenses after you retire, or even some late-in-life fun.

Using Life Insurance to Avoid Taxes

Many people think life insurance proceeds aren't taxable. Wrong! They don't count for income tax purposes, but proceeds paid to anyone other than your spouse or a charity do count toward your estate for estate tax purposes if you are both the insured person and the owner of the policy. And though the proceeds of a life insurance paid to, say, your spouse won't be taxed when you die (because of the marital deduction), the money augments her estate so that when she dies it may exceed the exemption threshold. To escape estate taxes, you must see that the policy is not owned by you as the insured, and that you have not retained incidents of ownership. There are two common ways to do this:

• **Third party owners.** With this first method, you take out a policy on your life that benefits your children or other beneficiaries.

Next—this is the critical move—you place ownership of the policy not in your name but in your beneficiaries' names—usually your children. Though you might have to structure the gifts carefully because of IRS scrutiny, you can give them enough money each year to pay the premiums, making sure to keep your total gift to each person below $10,000 per year to avoid the gift tax. As long as you live more than three years after transferring ownership, the policy is out of your estate.

• **Life insurance trusts.** These are a popular way of accomplishing the same goals. Here's how it works. A married couple has a combined taxable estate of $1,000,000 after using other tax-avoidance devices. They set up a life insurance trust in which the trust owns the policy on their lives—they do not. They can do this with an existing policy (by transferring ownership to the trust) or a new one. Each year, the husband makes transfers to the trust sufficient to pay the premiums. When he dies ten years later, the policy pays off $400,000—none of it taxable as a part of his gross estate—to the trust. The wife lives off the income from the trust. When she dies, the children take the principal remaining—again, tax-free.

New Tax Law Makes Estate Planning More Necessary

Mark Twain once responded to a premature obituary by remarking, "reports of my death have been greatly exaggerated." The same could be said of recent reports of the death of estate taxes. The Economic Growth and Tax Relief Reconciliation Act of 2001 does eliminate the estate tax, but for only one year. The federal estate tax will be with us in some form until the year 2010. Then it is repealed for a year, but just a year. Unless Congress acts, the estate tax goes back into effect in 2011. No one expects this law to go unchanged. Add in the many possibilities for changes in the way states assess estate taxes and it's clear that we have as much reason to plan our estates as before, if not more reason.

A Quick Summary

The new law goes into effect January 1, 2002. At that time, the estate tax will apply to taxable estates of $1 million or more, and the maximum rate of taxation will drop from 55% to 50%. The estate tax floor will rise in increments and the maximum estate tax rate will drop in increments (see table below) before the tax is repealed for a year in 2010.

Federal Exemptions Growing

Year	Exemption Amount For Estate Taxes	Highest Estate and Gift Tax Rates
2002	$1 million	50%
2003	$1 million	49%
2004	$1.5 million	48%
2005	$1.5 million	47%
2006	$2 million	46%
2007	$2 million	45%
2008	$2 million	45%
2009	$3.5 million	45%

CHAPTER NINE

Changing Your Mind

Changing, Adding to, or Revoking Your Will or Trust

LIFE DOES NOT stand still, and after you've crafted your initial estate plan, your circumstances are likely to change—you may have more children, acquire more assets, have a falling out with friends. Your children will grow up, you and your spouse may split up. And the law may change, making some of your estate planning obsolete or even counterproductive.

Most of these life changes will also occasion a change in your estate plan. It's a good idea to review your will or trust and your inventory of assets and recipients at least once a year to make sure everything is accounted for. Remember that this area of the law differs, often drastically, from state to state, so it's especially important to check (or have your lawyer check) how your state's law covers each of these procedures.

Codicils

You can change, add to, or even revoke your will any time before your death as long as you are physically and mentally competent to make the change. An amendment to a will is called a **codicil**. (It sounds like a prescription medicine, and you might think of it as a cure for an obsolete will.) You can't simply cross out old provisions in your will and scribble in new ones if you want the changes to be effective; you have to formally execute a codicil before witnesses, using the same formalities as when executing the will itself. Of course, it's vital that such codicils be dated so the court can tell whether they were made after your will was drafted. The codicil should be kept with the will. Since the same

DO I NEED TO UPDATE MY ESTATE PLAN? A CHECKLIST

Ask yourself if any of these changes have occurred in your life since you executed your will or trust.

- *Have you married or been divorced?*
- *Have relatives or other beneficiaries or the executor died or has your relationship with them changed substantially, with no provision in your will or trust for this contingency?*
- *Has the mental or physical condition of any of your relatives or other beneficiaries or of your executor changed substantially?*
- *Have you had more children or grandchildren, or have children gone to college or moved out of (or into) your home?*
- *Have you moved to another state?*
- *Have you bought, sold, or mortgaged a business or real estate?*
- *Have you acquired major assets (car, home, bank account)?*
- *Have your business or financial circumstances changed significantly (estate size, pension, salary, ownership)?*
- *Has your state law (or have federal tax laws) changed in a way that might affect your tax and estate planning?*

If you update your estate plan, you should also update your final instructions and will with the addresses and phone numbers of beneficiaries, trustees, executors, and others mentioned in estate-planning documents. It will make settling the estate much easier.

mental ability and freedom from undue influence is required for a codicil as for a will, if the changes are substantial it may be advisable to write a new will. It's a good idea to check with your lawyer before revising or revoking your will.

You also have to watch out for **ademption**, which is what happens if you will something (say, your antique automobile) to someone but by the time you die you no longer own it. In the case of the automobile, the gift would fail completely; the beneficiary wouldn't be entitled to another vehicle. (A good will avoids this by using language like "I give my antique Rolls-Royce to my son-in-law, Joe, but if I don't own it at the time of my death I give him a choice of any automobile I do own at the time of my death.")

Tangible Personal Property Memoranda

A **tangible personal property memorandum** (or **direction**) is a separate handwritten and/or signed document that is incorporated into the will by reference. (This means that the will says something like "This will incorporates the provisions of a separate Tangible Personal Property Memorandum. . . ." Then, the TPPM is regarded as part of the will.) The TPPM is dated and lists items of tangible personal property (e.g., jewelry, artwork, furniture) and the people you want the property to go to. Many states recognize the validity of such a signed instrument. Some require it to be in existence at the time the will is signed; others require it to be signed and witnessed as a will or codicil. For those states that do not give full effect to this type of document, the executor usually will attempt to comply as closely as possible with your desires, as indicated by the TPPM and your will. In those states, TPPMs are similar to **precatory** (i.e., advisory) gifts in your will or trust. Language is crucial here. If you don't direct that a certain asset go to a certain beneficiary but merely express a hope, wish, or recommendation that the asset be given, most courts would hold that this precatory language does not create a binding or legal obligation.

If you do use a TPPM, remember to provide for what happens to any of the property listed if the person who is in line to receive it should die before you do and you neglect to adjust the TPPM accordingly before your death.

To revoke a TPPM, you write "revoked" across each page of the old one, sign each page, and include the date of revocation. Attach the new TPPM to the will and make sure it's kept where it will be found after your death. If you have incorporated the TPPM in your will by reference, many states require you to amend the will to incorporate the amended document.

If you have a revocable living trust, you may give these items to the trustee to be distributed to the persons named in the trust. You can make changes by writing, signing, and dating amendments, without having them witnessed.

Revoking a Will

Sometimes when you undergo a major life change, such as divorce, remarriage, having more children, getting the last child out of the house, or even winning the lottery, it's a better idea to rewrite your will from scratch rather than making a lot of small changes through codicils. It's best to do this by executing a new will that states that it revokes the old one. There are two schools of thought about what to do about the old will. Some lawyers recommend that you destroy it, if possible in front of your lawyers and the witnesses of your new will. Others do not recommend destroying prior wills: A prior will is often very useful in avoiding arguments that there was undue influence. If there are a number of wills that have similar provisions, prior wills are often very good evidence.

When you write a new will, be sure to include the date it's signed and executed and put in a sentence that states the new will revokes all previous wills. Otherwise, the court is likely to rule that the new one only revokes the old where the two conflict, which could cause problems. If you keep an unsigned copy of the old will with the new one, write on each page "revoked, superseded by will dated ____." This provides a record in case any questions arise.

If you fail to change or rewrite your will to account for changes in your life, the courts will give as much effect to your old will as possible. Some changes may be accommodated by the law, regardless of what your will says. For example, if you have a new child and don't explicitly say you don't want her to inherit anything, then the law may give that child a share of your estate. Likewise, a new spouse. In some cases, though, assets that aren't accounted for go into the **residuary estate** (see chapter 3 for more). That's what's taken care of by a paragraph of most wills that says that you leave everything else to your spouse or St. Jude's hospital or whomever. It's more likely, though, that you want that hot new roadster you bought last year to go to your twenty-five-year-old son rather than to your seventy-year-old widow, and that's why it's best to modify your will periodically to account for such **after-acquired assets**.

Amending a Trust

Trusts are generally easier to amend than wills, requiring fewer formalities. You modify a trust through a procedure called **amendment**. You should amend your trust when you want to change or add beneficiaries, change disposition of assets in the trust, or change trustees. You amend a trust in a document, called an **amendment to the trust**, explaining the changes, specifying the new additions or deletions, signed by you and dated. You should not detach a page from the trust document, retype it to include the new information, and put it back in because this could invite a legal challenge from a disgruntled nonbeneficiary or require a court's construction of the trust.

You don't have to write a formal amendment to the trust to add property to it because a properly drafted trust will contain language giving you the right to include property acquired after the trust is drafted. You simply make sure the new property is titled as being owned by the trust and list it on the schedule of assets in the trust. You *do* have to amend the trust if the newly acquired property is going to a different beneficiary than the one already named in the trust or if the trust has more than one beneficiary listed.

It is awkward to revoke, not amend, your trust when making major changes. In some jurisdictions, you might have to transfer all assets out of the name of the trust back into your name and then retransfer them to the new trust. Even if the trustee makes the transfer him- or herself, it can be a cumbersome procedure. It's better to restate the trust in its entirety, with all changes in the restated version. This way, the original trust is simply amended and not destroyed and there is no need for further transfer of assets. The trust may retain its original date of creation. Occasionally, when a new trust has replaced an old one, someone will slip up and fail to transfer all the assets in the first trust to the new one. Restating a trust makes sure that all the assets remain in the trust and new ones are added. If you do revoke a trust, do so in a document, signed and dated by you, unless some other method is specified in the trust instrument. When you create a new trust to replace the revoked one, state at the beginning that it supersedes the trust dated———and signed by you.

Most lawyers say you should review your trust from time to time to ensure that it still meets your needs. It is advisable to go over it with your lawyer every three to five years or whenever a major change in your estate or family has occurred.

If you have a will that pours over to the trust, add a clause in the pourover provision that says "including all amendments made by me from time to time." Then, it will be unnecessary to make a new will or codicil each time you amend the trust.

Special Considerations for Living Trusts

If you have a living trust, remember that should you acquire property in your own name and die before you can put it into your living trust the property will automatically become part of your probate estate and will have to go through probate. If your will is properly drafted, such property will be picked up by your will's residuary clause (see chapter 3) and pass to the beneficiaries named there. That's why it's essential to have a will even if you have a living trust.

Other estate-planning documents you might want to keep up-to-date include IRAs, insurance policies, income savings plans such as 401(k)s, government savings bonds (if payable to another person), and retirement plans. You should keep a record of these documents with your will and update them as needed when you update your will.

■

CHAPTER TEN

Choosing the Executor or Trustee

ONE OF THE most important decisions you'll make is picking the person (or persons or institution) to be in charge of your assets after you're gone. That means the executor of your will and the trustee of any trusts you set up. (Another important decision, choosing a guardian for your minor children, is discussed in chapter 6; choosing an agent for your power of attorney is discussed in chapter 12.) The tasks of each of these **fiduciaries** (people who are legally obliged to act in your interests) differ slightly so we'll discuss the factors you should consider for each separately. But in choosing either, you must find someone with the proper balance of people skills and financial acumen.

You can choose more than one person to fulfill these duties: co-executors or co-trustees. This is a way to ensure that at least one person has legal or financial expertise and one is close to the family. If you choose this course, be sure to pick people or entities that can work together. You must also choose a successor in case your first choice dies or is unable to serve.

CHOOSING THE EXECUTOR

Who will be the person or institution responsible for administering your estate through probate? Chapter 11 spells out what the executor does, but the most important thing is that you pick someone who is financially responsible, stable, and trustworthy.

The law requires an executor because someone must be responsible for collecting the assets of the estate, protecting the estate property, preparing an inventory of the property, paying valid claims against the estate (including taxes), representing the estate in claims against others, and, finally, distributing the estate property to the beneficiaries. These last two functions may require liquidating assets; that is, selling items like stocks, bonds, even furniture, a car, or a residence to have enough cash to pay taxes, creditors, or beneficiaries. The will can impose additional duties not required by law on the executor: choosing beneficiaries or distributing personal property, even investing funds.

Sounds like a lot of work, doesn't it? It can be, and some of it can be complicated. However, the executor doesn't necessarily have to shoulder the entire burden. He or she can pay a professional out of the estate assets to take care of most of these functions, especially those requiring legal or financial expertise, but that will reduce the amount that goes to the beneficiaries. Therefore, handling an estate is often a matter of balancing expertise, convenience, and cost.

There's no consensus, even among lawyers, about who makes the best executor; it all depends upon your individual circumstances.

The Case for a Paid Executor

One approach is to appoint someone with no potential conflict of interest—that is, someone who doesn't stand to gain from the will. For this reason, many testators avoid naming family members or business partners. This helps avoid will contests from disgruntled relatives or associates who might accuse the executor of bias. If you have several beneficiaries who don't get along, you may want an outside executor who's independent of all factions. The larger the estate, the more the potential for conflicts, and the more you should consider naming an outside executor. You should also consider the possibilities of conflicts of interest if you have several beneficiaries.

Sometimes there are reasons for choosing a professional executor instead of your spouse. Your spouse may be incapacitated by grief, illness, or disability. Nonetheless, he or she as executor will be personally liable for unpaid estate taxes and fines for late filings, even if he or she has delegated such tasks to a lawyer.

Furthermore, since the executor must gather all the estate assets, your spouse may be faced with the odious duty of retrieving money or property you loaned to other friends.

If you think your spouse may not be up to the job (considering that he or she may also be saddled with sole responsibility for any minor children), you might choose a lawyer or other professional, even though it means paying a fee. Remember, this is a job that, primarily because of tax procedures, can take more than three years' involvement, though most estates take far less (and, in any event, the first few months are by far the hardest).

For larger estates, it's often advisable to use a lawyer or a bank. A complicated estate that involves temporarily running a business often demands an institutional fiduciary, such as a bank, that can call on the advice of lawyers, tax experts, accountants, investment counselors, even business administrators; it's impartial and immortal.

You might also consider hiring your lawyer as executor if you anticipate a will contest or know that the estate is going to require a lot of legal work.

The Case for an Unpaid Executor

Most of the time, when there is little possibility of a contest, the fees that lawyers and other paid executors charge may make it too expensive to hire such outsiders. Because of this expense, many people choose a friend or family member who will **waive** (decline) the executor's fee to which he or she would be entitled—and which comes out of your estate.

For people whose assets amount to less than half a million dollars or so, your spouse or a mature child (or children) may be your choice. An executor in this category will naturally be interested in making sure the probate process goes as quickly and smoothly as possible.

One compromise popular with small business owners is to appoint co-executors, such as one personal friend and one person with business expertise, and specify which executor will be responsible for which duties. Or to prevent family dissension, your will may provide that all of your children serve as co-executors. Co-executors can be a good idea if the main beneficiary lives in another state and it would be inconvenient for him or her to make frequent trips to handle clerical details; you could appoint another relative or friend who lives in the same city as the probate court to handle details locally. (George Washington appointed seven executors!)

What to Look for in an Executor

It's important to be sure the executor is capable of doing the job. Think of the appointment as employment—not a way to reward (or punish) a friend or a relative.

The quality most desirable in an executor is perseverance in dealing with bills (especially the hospital, Medicare, ambulance and doctor charges incurred in a last illness). Bills often require a lot of paperwork, first paying them, then being reimbursed by insurance companies. Pick someone who has the time and inclination to deal with bureaucrats and forms. Also, the executor may have to cope with relatives who may be wondering why it's taking so long to receive their inheritance or why their bequests are smaller than they expected. This can happen if, for example, the deceased's money was aggressively invested in the stock market and those stocks nose-dived after he wrote the will.

The executor must notify the IRS of his appointment by sending in Form 56 and applying for a separate taxpayer ID number for the estate, using Form SS-4. He must file Form 706 to pay the estate tax, for estates of gross value greater than the exemption amount ($1 million in 2002 and 2003), within nine months after the date of death. It is often advisable to file a return for an estate valued at less than the exemption amount if there is a reasonable possibility that the IRS may take the position that the value exceeds that amount.

Often, the executor must file a state estate tax return as well. On the federal estate tax return, there is a credit for state death taxes. That credit is paid directly to the state, a so-called pick-up tax.

Your executor must also file a final income tax return (Form 1040) for you by April 15 of the tax year after the year you died or obtain an extension. The estate receives a separate tax identification number, and any income to the estate of $700 or more in one year before the estate is completely settled is subject to income tax. The executor may select a fiscal year. It begins when the decedent dies. The last day is the last day of any of the eleven months immediately following the date of death, as selected by the executor. The fiscal year is often the calendar year for ease of accounting.

The executor can hire a CPA or lawyer to handle the tax returns. If the estate includes stocks or other investments, the executor may have to hire an investment adviser, particularly if the value of the estate has changed substantially because of changes in the market.

In most estates, no significant legal expertise is required to serve as executor; the issues are all financial. The executor will generally work with a lawyer to probate the will. Estate fees paid to the lawyer may be set by law (some states specify an hourly rate, some a fee based on a percentage of the estate). The lawyer handles all the court appearances and filings while the executor provides information and input.

The executor cannot be a minor or convicted felon. He or she must be a U.S. citizen. And while all states allow nonresidents to act as executors, some require a nonresident to be a primary beneficiary or close relative. Others require a surety bond or require that the out-of-state executor engage a resident to act as

BUT I DON'T WANT TO BE AN EXECUTOR!

*If you learn after a relative has died that you're named as executor and you don't want to serve, you should file a document with the court called a **declination**. If the will named a contingent executor (and if the deceased followed our instructions in the sample will, it did), he or she will take over; if none was named, the court will appoint one.*

If you are a family member who has been named executor—a surviving spouse, for example—you must take steps immediately to safeguard the estate assets against loss, fire, theft, and a sharply declining market. It may be costly to delay beginning the executor's duties until grief subsides. A competent lawyer can relieve many of the burdens of the executor.

his or her representative and to keep the assets in the state of primary probate.

Whomever you choose, be sure to provide in your will for a replacement executor in case the original executor dies or is unable or unwilling to act. Otherwise, the court will have to choose the replacement.

What if you also have a living trust? It's generally preferable to name the same person or institution as the executor and the trustee or successor trustee (see below). If you don't want to do this, discuss your reasons with your lawyer.

Giving the Executor More Powers

The law defines, and sometimes restricts, the powers of an executor. For this reason, it's often a good idea to specify in your will that your executor will have certain powers beyond those normally granted by state law. What powers should you give the executor? It depends on how much expertise he or she has in legal and financial matters, your state's law, and what your estate consists of. Many lawyers put some or all of the following powers into the boilerplate language of the wills they write for their clients:

RESPONSIBILITIES OF THE EXECUTOR

- *Guiding the will through probate to legal acceptance of its validity, including defending it against will contests.*
- *Collecting the assets of the deceased.*
- *Transferring legacies and gifts to the beneficiaries.*
- *Evaluating and paying claims against the estate, especially bills and taxes (see pages 135–36).*
- *Raising money to pay these claims, often by selling estate assets.*
- *Preparing and filing a budget and accounting for the court.*

- **Power to hire professional help.** You can state, in your will or final instructions letter, that you expect your executor to appoint a competent attorney and other appropriate counselors to speed the process of settling your estate. Besides taking the burden off your executor (especially important if it's your spouse) and bringing expertise to your estate administration, it will also forestall any second-guessing or complaints by relatives or beneficiaries about the money spent on hiring a lawyer or accountant.

- **Power to retain certain kinds of property in the estate.** This is necessary because state law may mandate that certain kinds of property be sold (e.g., "unproductive assets," which might be interpreted to include a family business that hasn't yet reached its full potential).

- **Power to continue running your business.** This will keep the business going until a new chief executive is chosen, unless you want it liquidated.

- **Power to mortgage, lease, buy, and sell real estate and other assets.** This ability is often limited by law if not otherwise specified in the will.

- **Power to borrow money.** This is usually to pay estate debts or taxes.

AN EXECUTOR WHO KNOWS HIS (AND YOUR) BUSINESS

If you run a business or are self-employed, consider making your executor or co-executor someone knowledgeable in your field. Sometimes the specialized knowledge of accounting or tax laws applicable to your area of business is easier for a colleague than for your spouse or other relative to master.

Take the example of a self-employed writer. Even in a profession notorious for its practitioners' lack of business acumen, certain specialized knowledge is often required. And some tasks must still continue after the writer is dead: recording copyrights, negotiating contracts for reissues of previously published material, deciding which publisher should (and equally important, which should not) get rights to reprint articles, determining which works should be completed by others, figuring out television and movie rights, deciding what happens to your manuscripts, letters, and other materials (perhaps a university or library or historical society would be interested in them) . . . there are many decisions to be made. Would your executor know how to handle them? If not, appoint a co-executor who does.

When you die, any records that are kept only in your head will go straight into the ground with you. Write it all down—and tell your heirs where it's written down (file folder, computer disk, etc.).

• **Power to take advantage of tax savings.** Exercising the various options permissible under tax law, such as filing a joint tax return with your surviving spouse, can save money.

If you do decide to appoint an interested person as the sole executor and give that person discretionary powers to determine who gets which assets, it may be wise to include a method for making these discretionary decisions. Arbitration by a third party can help avoid any abuse of discretion or placing pressure on the executor.

Executor's Commissions

In most states, an executor who is also a lawyer cannot receive both the attorney's fees and an executor's commission. In such cases, it's often to your advantage to use an attorney as executor; otherwise, if your nonlawyer executor must hire an attorney, your estate may pay both the executor's commission and the attorney's fee. Many attorneys will waive their executor's commission and take only the attorney's fees.

You can agree with your executor (either in a contract or the will itself) to fix an executor's fee that's different from that imposed by the state.

CHOOSING THE TRUSTEE

If your will leaves assets to a trust, the executor will transfer those assets to the trustee for distribution to the beneficiaries or for continued management. While an executor's duties can be onerous, at least in the absence of controversy they're over within at most a few years. A trustee's duties can continue for generations. And they require expertise in collecting estate assets, investing money, paying bills, filing accountings (quarterly or annually) and managing money for beneficiaries. The trustee consults with your beneficiaries about the size of the checks issued periodically, what expenses will be paid, what withdrawals against principal will be permitted. Obviously, then, it's preferable to choose someone with whom the beneficiaries feel comfortable. Since no individual lives forever, a bank or trust company should ultimately be designated as successor trustee.

What powers should you give the trustee? In general, it's a good idea to give wide latitude to the trustee because the economy changes so quickly. And because the law often limits what kinds of investments a trustee can make, you have to spell out these powers in the trust agreement.

A trust is a binding legal contract. The trustee—whether a bank or a relative—has a legal obligation to follow your instructions and to manage the trust funds in a reasonable and prudent manner. If the trustee mismanages the funds, any beneficiary can demand an accounting of how the money in the trust has been spent. If a beneficiary doesn't think the trustee acted reasonably, he or she can sue for reimbursement of any ill-gotten proceeds or improper losses and have the trustee removed from that position. However, the beneficiary will have to show more than, say, that stocks the trustee bought or retained lost money. The dissatisfied beneficiary has to show that investing in or retaining those stocks was unreasonable at the time.

The biggest decision to make in designating a trustee is whether to use a family member or a professional. Most (though not all) of the following discussion applies primarily to trusts other than living trusts; those are discussed separately at the end of this chapter.

Family Members as Trustees—Pros and Cons

Many people choose family members to serve as trustees. They don't charge a fee and they generally have a personal stake in the trust's success. If the family member is competent to handle the financial matters involved, has the time and interest to do so, and you're not afraid of conflict if a relative is named trustee, using a family member can be a good move for a small- to medium-sized trust. If you make a relative a trustee, be sure to consider who the successor will be in the event of death, incapacity, divorce, or other family strife.

Many grantors name co-trustees. Usually the spouse will be a co-trustee so that when one spouse dies, the other takes over. A corporate trustee, while an expert, may be too expensive for a moderate estate. Before selecting a trust company, it is advisable to discuss this with a trust officer of the institution.

The beneficiary himself may be named as trustee if he is an adult. If the trustee's powers are restricted to comply with federal estate tax law limitations, this arrangement may give the trustee/beneficiary control over the trust assets and avoid estate taxes after his death. However, it also subjects him to taxes on the income from the trust. Depending on the trust and the powers of the trustee, it might open the trust assets to attack from creditors. And the beneficiary probably won't have the professional familiarity with investments that a trust officer would—though, again, he can hire such help.

Here's the downside to choosing family members:

- **Lack of expertise.** Relatives often lack the financial acumen of a professional trust officer and so must often hire professional help.

- **Mortality.** Trusts can last for many years. Human trustees die; banks don't, and if they merge, the new bank automatically takes over the old bank's trust operations.

- **Family conflicts.** Depending on their relationship with the beneficiary, family trustees may have problems with what the beneficiary wants and what's best for him or her. Sibling rivalry may also complicate arrangements in which one brother or sister serves as trustee for others. A professional manager doesn't face such pressures.

An increasingly popular middle course between naming an institutional trustee and naming a family member is choosing a relative as trustee—and hiring a bank or investment company as an independent investment adviser rather than naming it as a co-trustee. It is familiar with the nuances of law and investment financing, and its fee for investment advice may be smaller than the one it charges to serve as a co-trustee. Often, for tax reasons, you would name both your beneficiary and another family member as co-trustees, then have the nonbeneficiary co-trustee hire the investment adviser.

Institutional Trustees—Pros and Cons

Banks are permanent institutions that can manage your trust for decades. They also have professional knowledge of and experience with investment options. They're objective and regulated by law. If you question the honesty, reliability, or ability of a friend or family member, a bank is the usual preference; and it can handle the investments, tax preparation, management, and accounting.

The disadvantages?

- **Cost.** If you do use a bank or trust company to manage the assets, expect to pay a fee for those services. These institutions sometimes have a minimum fee that makes them costly for a small trust. Ask your trust company for its schedule of fees or discuss it with a trust officer. Find out what services are included and those for which additional fees are charged, including any termination fee. Fees are deductible for income tax purposes to the extent the income is taxable to the trust or beneficiaries.

• **Conservatism.** Bank investments are generally conservative, with all the advantages and disadvantages that implies. While you, the grantor, can program the kind of investment strategy you want the professional trustee to follow, that can cause problems because of changed circumstances after your death.

• **Impersonality.** While a bank probably won't die, that doesn't mean your beneficiaries will always be dealing with the same person; personnel move around or move on. As depositors in many banks have learned, the bank itself can change hands. And your beneficiaries will want someone who is able and willing to listen to and discuss their needs and questions; impersonal institutions are sometimes weak in these interpersonal areas. On the other hand, when squabbling relatives are involved, impersonality can be a boon.

If you do choose an institutional trustee, make sure you and your beneficiaries are comfortable with the people they'll be dealing with.

Using a Lawyer as Trustee

If you pick a lawyer, he or she may charge by the usual hourly rate, which may prove less or more expensive than a bank's fee. Some firms have set up investment subsidiaries to handle the trustee business, but there's a possible conflict of interest there. If you choose a lawyer as trustee, ask to see his or her records of performance in investing and managing trust income.

A good rule of thumb: If the trust assets amount to more than a few hundred thousand dollars or there are any complicated problems, you should at least explore the option of using a professional trustee.

PICKING THE TRUSTEE IS A FAMILY AFFAIR

It's crucial that everyone in the family (not just the wage earner) see the fee schedule and other records of any professional trustee you're considering hiring so they can make an informed decision about who will make the best trustee. If the beneficiaries are old enough, they should be involved as well. After all, when the creator of the trust is enjoying eternal rest, they're the ones who'll have to live with this decision.

In choosing an institutional trustee, co-trustee, or investment adviser, your lawyer may be able to give you some names of such companies and may be willing to accompany you as you make the rounds, asking the trust officer the hard questions:

- *What are all the possible fees you charge?*
- *What is your record of rate of return on trust investments?*
- *What is the mechanism for changing the successor trustee?*
- *What happens if the person assigned to your trust account leaves the bank or trust company?*
- *What if the beneficiary needs emergency cash from the trust?*

You may be able to judge how responsive the company will be to your beneficiaries by their responses to such questions. The idea is to build a relationship with the bank so that it serves the beneficiaries' needs. You and the beneficiaries need to get to know the people you'll be working with.

A lot of people are intimidated by banks and large financial institutions, but since you're putting a lot of money in their care, you have a right to demand good service. Your lawyer should help you obtain it. If either your lawyer or the prospective professional trustee isn't responding to your needs, find a replacement. Remember, doing the hard work now will save your children or other beneficiaries much grief later.

Splitting the Difference: Co-trustees

Again, there's the possibility of splitting the job among several persons, professional and non-. You might pick someone who's good with investments, another who knows taxes, and a third who can talk to the beneficiaries. Usually the attorney for the trustees can handle the tax problems without being a co-trustee. Be aware that fiduciary tax returns can be complicated and the IRS likes to scrutinize them.

You (the grantor) can decide how the multiple trustees will make decisions; be sure to establish some mechanism for resolving disputes. Obviously, too many cooks can spoil the broth and you shouldn't make someone a trustee just to keep him or her from feeling left out; make sure that person can be useful.

The co-trustee should be familiar with the nuances of this particular trust. Also, be sensitive to present or potential conflicts between family members you're considering naming as co-trustees, particularly parents and children.

If you designate a family member as trustee, be sure to designate a successor co-trustee to take over after the original family member co-trustee dies or becomes incapacitated.

Warning: In some tax-saving trusts, the IRS prohibits using family members (especially spouses) as co-trustees. That's another reason you might want to have a lawyer's advice in naming a trustee.

Removing a Trustee

Some grantors write in a procedure for removing a trustee if the beneficiaries should become dissatisfied, but that also could let irresponsible beneficiaries circumvent your wishes to have the funds invested and maintained in a responsible manner. Such decisions depend on your relative confidence in the trustee and the beneficiaries.

Also, if you make it too easy for the grantor or beneficiaries to fire the trustee and step in to replace him or her, you might endanger the trust's tax advantages: The IRS might think that the grantor or beneficiary never really intended to give up control of

SHOULD THE GRANTOR OR BENEFICIARY BE A TRUSTEE?

The grantor of a revocable trust may serve as trustee, but the grantor of an irrevocable trust should never be a trustee as well. Not only will you almost always lose the tax benefits, you're inviting IRS scrutiny.

Should the trustee be a beneficiary? It depends. A beneficiary who is also a trustee may be liable for estate taxes, unless the trust is set up so as to avoid this. A key issue is whether to give beneficiaries the authority to make discretionary payments to themselves out of the trust principal or income. Such arrangements may limit the freedom to invest or pay out the trust principal. Generally, beneficiaries who are also trustees can only pay themselves principal for support, health, maintenance, and education based upon an ascertainable standard of living.

This may be a good situation for co-trustees: one can be the beneficiary, whose powers are limited to what the tax law allows; the other a disinterested trustee, maybe an institution, that can make those other decisions without jeopardizing tax advantages. Some states don't allow the sole beneficiary of a trust to be its sole trustee. Get your lawyer's advice before making a beneficiary a trustee.

the funds but could just fire and hire trustees until one did it the way the real power figure wanted. Solution? Omit removal power or give it to an outsider (such as your lawyer). And remember that removing a trustee can spark a legal fight, or at least a potentially expensive accounting.

TRUSTEES AND LIVING TRUSTS

In virtually all living trusts created primarily for probate avoidance or property management, the creator is also named the trustee. If it's a joint marital living trust, both spouses are frequently co-trustees; when the first spouse dies or becomes unable to act, the survivor becomes sole trustee.

If you depart from this pattern, you need to check with your lawyer. For example, making just one spouse the trustee of a

TAX-SAVING LIVING TRUSTS

If you are using the living trust primarily to avoid taxes, you should not make yourself the trustee. Instead, you may want to make the beneficiary the trustee or designate an independent trustee.

marital living trust can complicate things, as can naming a third party as trustee, which will require keeping separate trust and tax records and controlling the trustee's discretion. At the same time, don't feel as though you must be the trustee; you can designate a relative or friend with more time or knowledge than you—and you can always change your mind later.

When you create the trust, besides naming yourself trustee you should designate a successor trustee. Depending on the trust, the successor trustee distributes the trust assets to your beneficiaries after you die and/or continues to administer the trust for one or more generations. He or she could also take over management of the trust if you become incapacitated.

Whom should you choose? If the successor trustee is the primary beneficiary of the trust, he or she has the incentive to handle the transfers promptly and efficiently. However, it can be anyone you trust: a close friend, an adult child, your spouse, your lawyer, an accountant, or a corporate trustee.

A successor doesn't have to live in the same state that you do but it's usually more convenient if he or she does. You should take into account the amount of time and effort the successor will have to spend and his or her ability to perform the duties of the trustee and to deal with the beneficiaries.

If the successor merely is required to transfer property to the beneficiaries, a copy of the original trust agreement and death certificate of the original trustee should be sufficient for banks, stockbrokers, government agencies, and other entities that control the assets to enable them to be transferred to the successor or beneficiaries entitled to receive them. Sometimes, especially when real estate is involved, the successor trustee will have to sign over deeds transferring property from the living trust to the beneficiaries.

DUTIES OF THE SUCCESSOR TRUSTEE

Usually the successor trustee will be taking over for the creator of the trust, who may also be the original trustee. Therefore, some of the duties are similar to those of an executor. The duties will vary with the nature of the trust property and, of course, also depend on whether the original trustee has died or become disabled. As successor trustee, you should:

- *Know the contents of the trust agreement, which should spell out specific duties and instructions.*
- *Obtain a medical opinion confirming the original trustee's incapacity (if he has become disabled); or*
- *Obtain a copy of the death certificate (if the original trustee has died). Be sure to make several copies of these documents; the funeral home will obtain duplicate certified copies of death certificates.*
- *Notify the lawyer who prepared the trust of the original trustee's death or incapacity and explain that you are now the trustee.*
- *Inform any banks holding trust assets that you are now trustee.*

However, there are circumstances in which you will want the successor trustee to have more expertise, or at least the ability to hire professional help. For example, if any of your beneficiaries are minors or disabled or the trust is to continue, the successor will have to manage the trust property until they reach the ages at which you specified the property would be distributed to them or to their **remaindermen** (i.e., those who have a future interest in the trust). This may involve preparing tax returns, investing funds, and so on.

How about naming co-successor trustees? The discussion above can give some guidance here. When children are beneficiaries of the living trust, parents often choose to make them all equal co-beneficiaries, and therefore it makes sense to name them co-successor trustees as well. However, if you fear the children may fail to agree or it is impracticable to administer the

- Notify all entities that control pensions, insurance, or government benefits.
- Tell the family that you are the successor trustee.
- Send copies of the trust agreement to the beneficiaries.
- Inventory the trust property. (You'll need a list of the property, keys to any dwellings, businesses, or storage areas, and the like).
- Take care of business transactions as needed if the original trustee has become incapacitated.
- Be sure that you have adequate insurance to cover any possible liability you might incur as trustee and any loss or damage to property of the trust.
- Collect and pay all bills and taxes.
- Keep accounts of money paid out and income received.
- Hire a lawyer or an accountant to prepare any tax returns, if necessary.
- Distribute the property to beneficiaries in the order indicated in the trust agreement. Obtain receipts.
- Make a final accounting record and send copies to the beneficiaries.

trust with a number of trustees, this can be a bad idea. You may have to choose one child as trustee or put in a mechanism (such as arbitration) for resolving conflicts between co-successors. In any case, be sure to have a lawyer advise you if you fear such conflicts.

Frequently, conflicts or the size or complexity of the trust make an independent trustee necessary, such as a lawyer or trust company. Since no individual can be certain to serve for the duration of the trust, a trust company should always be designated as ultimate successor trustee; otherwise, an expensive court proceeding may be necessary to appoint a successor.

You have to specify the successor's powers, which will normally be broadly phrased: the ability to transfer assets to people or institutions, to pay debts and taxes, and to spend trust principal for maintenance, education, support, and health care. Be sure to get a lawyer's advice if you feel the need to control the powers of the successor trustee or the beneficiaries. Your lawyer can help write into the agreement special rules that will carry out your wishes.

In any event, don't forget to name an alternate successor trustee in case your first choice dies before you or otherwise is unwilling or unable to serve.

CHAPTER ELEVEN

■

Planning Now to Make Things Easier for Your Family

YOU'LL WANT to minimize your relatives' distress during the trying months after your departure. First, we'll discuss what actions you can take *now* to ease the burden on the family after you die. Then we'll take a brief look at probate to help you decide whether you should try to avoid or minimize probate proceedings.

YOUR FINAL INSTRUCTIONS

You can make your survivors' task easier by leaving a letter containing burial instructions and your other last wishes in a place where your family can find it.

The most important decision is what to spend on a funeral. The average funeral cost these days runs between $4,000 and $10,000, one of the largest single expenses a family incurs. Unfortunately, a grieving family may be pressured by the funeral director to spend more than it can really afford "to show how much you loved the departed."

To protect your estate and survivors from this sort of pressure, set a limit on funeral expenses and arrange the service while you're alive (through a funeral home) with the help of someone you trust, like your spouse, executor, or religious adviser. Funeral homes are legally required to send you a written

FUNERAL SERVICES

These are some of the options funeral homes may offer. Find out how much each home charges for each service, pick the ones that fit your needs and budget, and purchase a plan that provides them. It will save your loved ones needless turmoil and expense. You can join a memorial society now that will help you plan your own funeral and burial options. Some offer "preneed" plans (oh, the euphemisms for the D-word) that allow you to prepay funeral costs.

- *Burial, cremation, or gift of body for science.*
- *Transporting the body to the funeral home.*
- *Embalming and other preparation of the body.*
- *Selecting flowers.*
- *Selecting headstone, plaque, and interment site.*
- *Providing a hearse for the body and limousines for the family.*
- *Renting facilities for viewing the body.*
- *Memorial cards and guestbook.*
- *Transporting the body to the cemetery.*
- *Tents and chairs for the funeral.*
- *Copies of the death certificate.*
- *Assistance in notifying insurance companies, newspapers, and organizations the deceased belonged to.*

Other choices you'll have to make:

- *Open or closed casket?*
- *Indoor memorial service or graveside service (or both)?*
- *Elaborate or simple service?*
- *Who conducts the service: family member, religious adviser, funeral home?*
- *Who speaks at the service?*
- *Should music be played? If so, what music?*

price list—use it to comparison shop. The options range from basic cremation to elaborate memorial ceremonies (see box on page 152.) If you get a prepaid or "preneed" plan, make sure you sign a "fixed-price contract"; if you don't, your family could be surprised by charges above the amount you've already paid.

Warning: If your body will be transported out of the state in which you die, a permit may be required. The funeral home or health department can advise your survivors. Most states have laws concerning embalming, cremation, and so on. Occasionally, an unscrupulous funeral director will falsely tell survivors that the law requires certain procedures (such as purchase of a casket before cremation). So it's a good idea for you or your lawyer to research these requirements before you die and make sure your survivors know them.

Remember, oral or written instructions about burial aren't legally binding on your family or executor. The spouse or next of kin is entitled to handle burial arrangements; if no one comes forward to do so, state law takes over.

The instructions should list:

• What you want done with your body—buried, cremated, or donated to science. Funeral arrangements—information about any funeral plan you've bought or any account you've set up to pay burial expenses. Location of cemetery and burial plot. Location of service, clergy person or others you wish to speak, music, flowers, etc.

• Name of any charity or cause to which you wish contributions sent in your name.

• Location of your will and the identity and phone number of the executor and/or lawyer handling it.

• Location of your safe-deposit box, the key, and any important records *not* located in it, such as birth certificate; pre-/postnuptial, marriage, and divorce documents; important business, insurance, and financial records; pension and benefit agreements.

- Inventory of assets (see appendix), including documents of debts owed and loans outstanding, credit card and car information, post office box and key, information on any investments, deed to home, list of contents of household, IRA, pension, and bank accounts, list of expected death benefits, etc.

- Important information: names, addresses, dates, and places of birth for you and your spouse and family members (including ex-spouses, if any), Social Security numbers for you and your spouse and dependent children (and location of Social Security card), policy numbers and phone numbers and addresses of insurance companies and agencies that control your death benefits (employer, union, Veterans Affairs office, etc.).

- Name and address of your lawyer, executor, and employers.

- Information you want included in your obituary.

Where should you keep these instructions? Not with your will; sometimes a will isn't read until after the funeral. And not in a safe-deposit box, because it might be sealed pending reading of the will. You should keep a copy with your will, give copies to your lawyer, the will's executor, your spouse, and any other close family members or beneficiaries. The main thing is that it be accessible and that everyone who needs it will know in advance where to find it.

Cushioning the Blow

Many people are as concerned with sparing their survivors grief and stress as they are with dying itself. Especially in families where one spouse is the primary wage earner, the loss of income from that spouse's death can be as devastating financially as the death is emotionally. For that reason, your estate planning should include some provision for an emergency fund for your survivors, to tide them over the period immediately following your death. As discussed in chapter 2, life insurance is one method for doing this but there are others. A Totten trust or marital trust (see chapter 4) will provide your spouse with income on your death. And some states have pay-on-death accounts that can accomplish the purpose (see chapter 2). However, be aware that states sometimes freeze certain kinds of jointly held bank accounts until state tax authorities can assess their value. Some state laws allow the spouse to receive some or all of the funds within a few days of death, but others do not. Lesson: When planning your estate, find out your state's law and make sure your survivors have some freezeproof method of getting hold of money during whatever the period of delay is in your state.

Finally, you might locate now the name of a counselor or psychiatrist to help your family cope with grief. They don't have to call but at least they'll know that help is there. You might also put the names of local or national support groups for the newly bereaved in your list of final instructions; if you can't find one in the phone book or from friends, contact the American Association of Retired Persons.

Other Considerations

Note to husbands: Some widows sometimes find it hard to obtain credit after a husband dies, especially if they've worked in the home throughout their married life. Therefore, before you die, add her name to any credit cards currently held in your name only. After you die, your widow should notify credit card companies of your death and change all cards held in your joint names to her name alone. After your death, she should pay any debts that are owed jointly by you and herself (e.g., mortgage, utility bills) to shore up her credit rating.

Insurance policies demand special attention. If you were covered through a health plan provided by your employer, your spouse and dependent children may be entitled to continue that coverage for up to three years; check with your employer and leave written instructions. They may need to buy more insurance, or reduce the amount of life insurance now that you're gone. They will also need to change beneficiaries of their policies if you were one of them.

Families can fight over things as trivial as a favorite lamp or a wedding dress just as easily as valuable antiques or jewelry. That's why, as much trouble as it seems now, you'll be doing everyone a favor if you make a list (sometimes called a **precatory list** because it's not necessarily legally binding but is easily changeable) of personal property items that are too inexpensive (and change too often) to put in the will. Out to the side, put the name of the person whom you want to inherit each item—who gets what. (See also the discussion of tangible personal property memoranda in chapter 9.)

You might also need to think about what will happen to personal or business items that will outlast you. The widow of Sir Richard Francis Burton, the great explorer and translator of the *Arabian Nights*, burned all his unpublished manuscripts—to the anguish of scholars and adventure lovers ever since. Franz Kafka's dying injunction to his friend to burn his manuscripts was fortunately ignored; that's the only reason his legacy has come down through history. One of the sons of Johann Sebastian Bach sold many of his father's irreplaceable manuscripts to support his drinking; a descendant of Thomas Jefferson used some of Jefferson's private papers for kindling.

Few of us will reach the exalted status of these men. But you might want to consider whether a local university, library, museum, or other institution would be interested in your stamp collection, private correspondence with Vanna White, or other items of potential historical import. Your heirs and executors may not appreciate their value to posterity, so be sure to spell out what you want to happen to such items.

PROBATE

Probate (i.e., "probate of the will" or "admitting the will to probate") is the court-supervised legal procedure that determines the validity of your will.

The word "probate" is also used to mean "probating your estate." In this sense, probate is the process by which assets are gathered, applied to pay debts, taxes, and expenses of administration, and then distributed to those designated as beneficiaries in the will. The purpose of probate, put bluntly, is to take the ownership of your assets out of your dead hands and put them into those of a living person or an institution.

We can't discuss the process in detail—there are books on the subject and the court in your area may provide guidance to your executor. Instead, this discussion will center on how probate affects you now in your estate planning.

Thanks to the title of a book written some years ago—*How to Avoid Probate*—the only thing many people think about probate is that it should be shunned if at all possible. But times have changed and so has the process of probate in most states—so much that it's seldom the expensive, time-consuming beast it once was. For some people, avoiding probate should be the primary goal of their estate plan, and this book provides advice on how to do that where appropriate. But for many other families, especially those of moderate means, it can actually be more trouble to avoid probate than to go through it.

Even more than other aspects of estate planning, the details of probate vary by state. Ask your lawyer if avoiding probate should be one of your principal estate-planning goals.

Supervised or Unsupervised?

There are now essentially two kinds of estate administration in many states: supervised administration (for contested estates) and independent or unsupervised administration (for uncontested estates). (For variations, see box on page 158). A supervised administration requires court approval for some of the major steps in settling the estate. Independent or unsupervised administration allows the executor to take most of those steps without court permission. In one state, for example, unsupervised administration, called "independent administration," is available irrespective of the size of the estate. It requires one court appearance on admission of a will to probate and issuance of letters of office and—unless a contest develops over the will, a claim against the estate, or the accounting of the representative—a final report and the discharging of the representative.

Some states allow unsupervised administration if requested in the will; if your state is one and you trust your executor, be sure to provide for it in your will. The threshold for unsupervised administration in states that allow it varies. In some states, it is available to estates of all sizes; in others, it's available as long as

KINDS OF PROBATE

- **Supervised.** *The most formal and expensive method. The court plays an active role in approving each transaction. In states where it's optional, supervised administration is used when an estate is contested, when an interested party requests it, or when the executor's ability is questioned.*

- **Unsupervised or independent.** *A simpler, cheaper method in which the number of duties and procedures is reduced and the court's role is diminished or eliminated. It's used for estates that exceed the asset limit for small-estate administration (see below) but don't require heavy court supervision. It often requires consent of all beneficiaries, unless the will specifically requests unsupervised administration.*

- **Small-estate.** *The simplest and fastest method of transferring property at death other than joint tenancy or payable on death accounts and policies. A small-estate affidavit is available for estates ranging from $1,000 to $100,000, depending on state law. This approach is particularly advantageous where the bulk of the estate is in a trust and only an automobile or small bank account is in the name of the decedent at the time of death. No court administration is required.*

the executor is the only beneficiary. But some states have a tight dollar limit. In Maryland, for instance, the dollar cap is $20,000. In California, the estate can be no larger than $60,000; if it's larger, or contains more than $10,000 of California real estate, the court must supervise. Obviously, these limits exclude most estates from the easy unsupervised procedures.

Still, supervised administration, while time-consuming, seldom requires a lawyer's expertise, at least for moderate-sized estates. (In most larger estates, a lawyer might be needed.) Most probate proceedings are relatively routine, about as exciting as filing a tax return. The executor just has to be sure to complete the various forms, appraisals, and inventories required and obtain court approval before selling or distributing certain assets or paying debts.

If your estate is relatively modest, your probate court accommodating, and your state laws congenial, a levelheaded relative can probably handle probate. This is something that ought to be determined (preferably with the help of your estate-planning lawyer) before you die.

And there is good news if you're in one of the categories of people who can profit from probate avoidance techniques like living trusts or such other nonprobate transfers of property as joint tenancy or life insurance. Even though you still need a will, it's likely to be so simple and dispose of so little property (most of your assets will be distributed through your living trust or joint tenancy) that the cost and time it takes to see it through probate will be minimal.

In independent (unsupervised) administration, once the will is admitted to probate, the executor still has to complete the basic tasks of administration; he or she just doesn't have to report to the probate court. In some states, the executor must have the written consent of all interested parties to undertake an unsupervised administration and must file these forms with the application to open the estate. Once the testamentary letters have been issued, the executor can settle and close the estate without further intervention from the court. The final inventory and accounting must be sent to the beneficiaries, not the court.

If You Don't Have a Will

You can't avoid probate by not having a will. Even if you don't write a will (i.e., if you die intestate), you'll still have one—the one the state writes for you. The court will appoint a personal representative to serve as the administrator. This is usually a close relative or heir. The administrator's job is essentially the same as the executor's; the only difference is that he or she is appointed by the court instead of being selected by you in your will, and the administrator will probably be required to give a surety bond, whereas a will can waive surety and save a large bond fee. Probate will take place, but will cost more and take more time because you didn't leave instructions.

TEN FACTORS THAT REDUCE THE COST OF PROBATE

The more of these questions answered yes, the less probate should cost.

1. Has the estate been planned as indicated in this book?

2. Is the will up-to-date, self-proving, and properly prepared, with bequests made in a clear, simple, predictable manner?

3. Have you prepared an inventory of all your assets for your executor?

4. Is the fair market value of all the probate assets below the available exemption amount ($1 million in 2002 and 2003)?

5. Is there only one beneficiary of the will?

6. If there is a surviving spouse, are all the children also the children of the surviving spouse?

7. If your state has simplified (small-estate or unsupervised) probate procedures, does the fair market value of the estate fall below the ceiling for those procedures?

8. Is the probate estate free of real estate holdings in another state or a family business?

9. Was the estate plan discussed with the family and other beneficiaries before death?

10. Can the estate debts and taxes be resolved without delay or controversy?

HOW TO SAVE MONEY IN PROBATE

For most people, it's seldom necessary to use a lawyer as the sole executor. Instead, the preferred course is to allow the nonlawyer (usually family member) executor to do most of the work, which is gathering information and records. The executor files the required forms, figures and pays the taxes, and distributes the estate assets. If the executor has any questions, he or she can consult the lawyer. The executor may also pay the lawyer to review final documents for legal accuracy or do a few specific tasks that he or she can do best.

For some estates, this takes no more than a few hours of a lawyer's time. It's the single best way to save money in probate, but it does mean a trade-off for the executor: his or her time for the sake of your estate's money. Only you and your executor can decide whether the trade-off is worth it under the circumstances.

If you live in a state that assesses probate fees based on the value of the estate, it may be to your advantage to get property out of your estate by use of a living trust, joint tenancy, gifts, and so on. This tactic, along with setting your own financial affairs in order before you die, will also reduce the billable hours an attorney for the estate will have to charge. Prepare your own inventory before you die. After you die, your executor (if a family member who's waived a fee) should do as much of the work as possible, such as updating your inventory and notifying creditors.

AVOIDING PROBATE

It's no accident that for years one of the best-selling nonfiction books was titled *How to Avoid Probate.* But the need to avoid probate has been lessened in recent years as simplified procedures (such as the independent executor provisions) of some states have reduced or eliminated many of the hassles and charges. Though delays are possible, the average estate under the available exemption amount completes the probate process in six to nine months, depending on state law. And the reformed probate procedures in many states now make it possible for your spouse, minor children, and disabled children to obtain the money they need to live on almost immediately without waiting for the entire estate to clear probate.

Despite its sometimes cumbersome nature, probate does help ensure that those—and only those—entitled to take part of your estate do so. It reduces the time for creditors to present claims against the estate. While it's a public proceeding, how many of us are really worried about someone's going through our estate records? Probate privacy, though highly touted by living trust salespersons, is usually the concern of celebrities and the very rich, not the rest of us.

For most people, the complexity of the probate procedures of the state you live in is probably the single most important factor in deciding whether to use probate avoidance techniques. Probate isn't all bad, but if you can minimize the court's involvement, you should, especially if you live in a state that doesn't have alternative or simplified procedures or your estate doesn't qualify for them.

If you do intend to save money by avoiding probate, be sure to use one of the methods outlined in this book. Remember, you can avoid probate through

- Property in a trust

- Property that's jointly held (but *not* community property) or property payable on death to a designated person

- Death benefits from insurance policies, the government, and employers as well as other benefits controlled by contract

- Property given away before you die

Probate avoidance probably means seeing a lawyer. Please don't make the mistake so many people eager to avoid probate have—using one-size-fits-all estate forms from a book or computer program that don't take into account all your estate-planning needs (such as providing for your family) and the peculiarities of your individual situation.

CHAPTER TWELVE

■

When You Can't Make the Decision

Living Wills, Powers of Attorney, and Other Disability Issues

MOST OF US think of estate planning as something that really doesn't bear fruit until we're dead. But technology has changed all that. Modern medicine can now keep alive indefinitely many people who would have died a few years ago. Though alive, however, they may not necessarily be able to take care of themselves. Nowadays, a good estate plan must take into account the possibility that you may someday be unable to care for yourself, make decisions, or even regain consciousness—but remain alive.

You may remember the Nancy Cruzan case in which a Missouri woman injured in an auto accident suffered a head injury that rendered her unlikely to escape from an unresponsive, coma-like state. She had left no written instructions about what doctors were to do if she ever became so disabled. Her family wanted to discontinue intravenous feeding but the hospital—and the state—refused to allow it. Finally, in June 1990, the United States Supreme Court ruled that although individuals do have the right to refuse medical treatment, they must express their wishes clearly enough to meet the standards set by the state in which they live.

The case of Jack Kevorkian, the Michigan doctor who assists people in committing suicides, indicates just how touchy and ambivalent our society remains about euthanasia (mercy killing) and the right to die.

Let's hope that you never have to face the choices that the Cruzan family and Kevorkian's patients faced. But there are more common and less spectacular cases in which you may have to let someone else make important decisions for you because you aren't able to do so.

Twenty years ago, half of Americans died in institutions like hospitals or nursing homes; today, it's four out of five. The medical personnel in these institutions will look to you and/or your family for instruction on whether to revive you should the need arise. If such procedures would only mean great pain for you and prolonged anguish for your family or would leave you in a vegetative state, you might not want them performed. But you might not be in any condition to refuse them. Or you may be in a situation in which you want to live but can't manage your affairs.

The courts have ruled that all mentally competent adults have the right to refuse medical care. If you're in a condition in which you can't communicate and there is clear evidence of your wishes regarding treatment (such as a living will), those intentions must be obeyed. But the details get messy because state laws vary widely on the subject. As a practical matter, your instructions must be written down, preferably in a formal document, if there is to be a good chance they will be obeyed. Even then, there's no guarantee.

What you're trying to avoid is the agonizing situation of your partner or children gathered around your hospital bed asking each other and your doctor, "What would she want us to do?"—and your being unable to tell them.

There are some planning tools that can help. For financial matters, you can use trusts and durable powers of attorney to help you manage. For health-care decisions, some states have **family consent laws** permitting other family members to make some health-care decisions on your behalf. But in most states, no one, not even your spouse, has the legal right to make any kind of decision on your behalf; they might have to file a court petition to get it, and obtaining such guardianships or conservatorships can be expensive, time-consuming, and still not accomplish your wishes.

As a result, most states have adopted various other legal devices to help your wishes be carried out when you're incapable of making such important decisions. In considering these "lifetime planning" or "advance directive" documents, remember that they're only valid if made while you are competent—not when you've entered an advanced state of, say, Alzheimer's disease. Also, state laws about how these documents must be created and witnessed vary greatly. With some, it's just a matter of filling in the blanks on a form; with others, you need a lawyer's help.

In most states, lawyers recommend that you make out both a living will and a durable power of attorney for health care, tell your doctor and lawyer about these decisions, and give them a copy of each document to keep on file. It's also a good idea to give a copy to the executor of your regular will. Even where states don't accept some of these tools as legally binding, they carry substantial moral weight with doctors and health-care providers.

This chapter outlines some of the methods you can plan right now to manage your affairs when you might not be able to make decisions regarding your property, your medical treatment, even your life.

MANAGING YOUR PROPERTY

If you should become disabled, life goes on. Bills (rent, mortgage, utilities) must be paid. Form 1040 must be filed. If you own a business, you may want it to carry on without you. Your property must be managed.

You may expect your spouse to do all this for you, but what if he or she is killed or disabled in the same event that renders you unable to manage your affairs? What if your spouse dies before you do? What if your spouse is simply not capable of handling your affairs? An estate plan must anticipate such situations.

Joint Tenancies and Living Trusts

One way to give someone else authority to manage your property is to put it into joint tenancy. This will give your co-owner the power to handle your property should you become disabled. In some cases (usually when a spouse is a joint tenant), this arrangement may be all you need to protect your property.

In many cases, though, such joint tenancies are a bad idea, or at least insufficient to take care of all possibilities; chapter 2 explains why. For families with sufficient assets, a better method is to use a revocable living trust (see chapter 5). You name yourself and someone you trust as co-trustees, transfer the assets that need managing (especially things like investments, rental property, and bank accounts) to the trust, and give the co-trustee the powers over the assets you designate. You can, for example, require that until you are incapacitated he or she obtain your approval before taking any action. If you become incapacitated, your co-trustee will manage the assets for you. When you die, the assets can pass into your estate, continue in the trust, or be paid to a beneficiary.

A properly written living trust is much more flexible than a power of attorney. However, a revocable living trust may not be appropriate for your situation. And a revocable living trust can interfere with your eligibility for Medicaid assistance in paying for nursing home care, should you be eligible for it (see the discussion of Medicaid planning that concludes this chapter). An *irrevocable* trust can encourage your family and friends to make donations for your care. It can help cover needs not met by public entitlements like Medicaid without disqualifying you from receiving them, but such a trust must be very carefully drafted.

Durable Powers of Attorney

For many people, a **durable power of attorney (DPA)** is the best protection against the consequences of becoming disabled. A DPA is a document in which one person (the **principal**) gives legal authority to another person (the **agent**) to act on the principal's behalf. State laws vary, but a DPA generally has to be signed and notarized and state that it shall be "durable"—that is, that it will become effective and will continue in effect after you become incapacitated. It terminates when you die, when you cancel it (you can cancel it at any time), or at a time you specify.

The DPA lets you appoint an agent (usually your spouse or child) to manage all or part of your business or personal affairs. The law does impose the responsibility on the agent to act as your **fiduciary**, but it might be difficult for you or your family to take him or her to court. Since this person can in effect do anything with your money, you should be sure to appoint someone you trust and in whose judgment and ability you have confidence.

A DPA's flexibility is one of its main advantages. You can limit the authority of the agent in the document, giving him or her as many or as few powers over your property as you wish, attaching conditions and so on. You should check with an attorney before executing a DPA.

MAKING TREATMENT DECISIONS

You now have several ways to prepare for the possibility that you may sometime be unable to decide for yourself what medical treatment to accept or refuse. This section discusses health-care powers of attorney, living wills, and health-care advance directives (which permit you to create a health-care power of attorney and living will in one document). See appendix on page 203 for a sample health-care advance directive prepared by the American Bar Association, the American Medical Association, and the American Association of Retired Persons (AARP).

Health-Care Powers of Attorney

Remember, federal law now gives you the right to consent to or refuse any medical treatment and to receive information about the risks and possible consequences of a given procedure, advance directives (such as living wills), and life-sustaining medical care and your right to choose whether to receive it. No one else, not even a family member, has the right to make these kinds of decisions unless you've been judged incompetent (see "Guardianships" on page 173) or are unable to make such decisions because, for example, you're in a coma or it's an emergency situation. No one can force an unwilling adult to accept medical treatment even if it means saving his or her life.

Society has gradually come to a rough consensus on these principles, and almost all medical providers follow them. Difficulties still arise when your wishes or intentions aren't clear. That's where these planning tools come in.

A special kind of durable power of attorney called a **health-**

QUESTIONS TO ASK YOURSELF BEFORE MAKING ADVANCE DIRECTIVES

1. What are my values?

These documents are tools to make sure your wishes are carried out. Some of the issues to explore (perhaps with your family, friends, minister, or doctor) include:

- How important is independence and self-sufficiency in my life?
- What role should doctors and other health professionals play in medical decisions that affect me?
- What kind of living environment is important to me?
- What role do religious beliefs play in these decisions?
- How should my family and friends be involved (if at all) in these decisions?

2. Who should be my agent?

This is the person who will make decisions about health-care for you if you become incapacitated. Who can you trust to know what you would want if unexpected circumstances arise? Who will be able to handle the stress of making such decisions? (Remember, state laws sometimes prevent doctors and others from acting as agents in these circumstances.)

3. What guidelines should I impose?

You don't have to spell out every contingency; in fact, you need to leave your agent some flexibility if the unexpected happens. But if you have specific intentions (not being kept alive by feeding tubes if you are brain-dead, for example), you can help your agent by writing them down.

4. How can I deal with reluctant doctors?

The medical establishment has been slow to recognize patients' rights to make these kinds of decisions in advance. If you have a regular physician or hospital, you might want to discuss these issues with them now to make sure your wishes, and those of your agent, will be carried out.

care power of attorney (HCPA) is used to deal with health-care planning. It allows you to appoint someone else to make health-care decisions for you—including, if you wish, the decision to refuse intravenous fluids or feeding or turn off the respirator if you're brain-dead—if you become incapable of making that decision. The form can be used to make decisions about things like nursing homes, surgeries, and artificial feeding.

Obviously, decisions so important should be discussed in advance with your agent, who should be a spouse, child, or close friend, and you should try to talk about various contingencies that might arise and what he or she should do in each case. A copy should be put in your medical record. Since it's so much more flexible than a living will, the HCPA is a very useful document that could save you and your family much anxiety, grief, and money.

You can revise or revoke the HCPA, living will, or health-care advance directive at any time, including during a terminal illness, as long as you are competent. To change or revoke these documents, notify the people you gave the copies to, preferably in writing.

It's a good idea to prepare the DPA, HCPA, and living will (see below) all at once and make sure they're compatible with each other and the rest of your estate plan. Since a health-care advance directive combines the HCPA and living will, it automatically assures their compatability. These days, all these documents should be regarded as essential components of any estate plan. Some attorneys advise using different people to serve as agents under your HCPA and DPA. The former is usually a spouse, child, or close relative who can make health-care decisions; the latter a lawyer or other money-wise friend, relative, or professional competent to make business and financial arrangements. You can terminate the HCPA at any time.

Pulling the Plug: Living Wills

A living will is a written declaration that lets you state in advance your wishes about the use of life-prolonging medical care if you become terminally ill and unable to communicate, persistently vegetative, or irreversibly comatose. It lets your wishes be carried out even if you become unable to state them. If you don't want to burden your family with the medical expenses (the last month of life averages almost $20,000) and prolonged grief involved in keeping you alive when there's no reasonable hope of revival, a living will typically authorizes withholding or turning off life-sustaining treatment if your condition is irreversible.

The living will comes into play when you are incapable of making and communicating medical decisions. Usually you'll be in a such a condition that if you don't receive life-sustaining treatment (intravenous or tube feeding, respirator), you'll die. If the living will is properly prepared and clearly states your wishes, the hospital or doctor must abide by it and, in turn, will be immune from criminal or civil liability for withholding treatment. Some people worry that by making out a living will, they are authorizing abandonment by the medical system, but a living will can state whatever your wishes are regarding treatment. So even if you prefer to receive all possible treatment, whatever your condition, it's a good idea to state those wishes in a living will.

Almost all states now have living will laws, but they are far from uniform. There are two kinds of living wills: **statutory** (for states that have forms in their living will laws) and **nonstatutory** (for those that don't). Most of the states have so-called right-to-die laws, but provisions vary from state to state and can be expected to change in coming years. In fact, some lawyers believe that people in certain states would be better off without a living will, since the statutory form forbids doctors from withdrawing nutrition and hydration (i.e., feeding tubes)—a restriction you probably don't want. Many lawyers believe that power of attorney for health care is preferable to a living will. In any event, get sound legal advice before proceeding.

A statutory living will tracks the language in the law of your state and leaves little room for uncertainty if properly prepared. A nonstatutory living will follows generally accepted principles about the right to die and refusal of treatment.

The form required for a valid living will differs in each state. Be sure to check with a lawyer or find out about your state's law by contacting: Choice in Dying, 1-800-989-WILL; www.choices.org.

IF I HAVE A LIVING WILL, DO I STILL NEED A HEALTH-CARE POWER OF ATTORNEY?

Absolutely. That's why the health-care advance directive combines them.

- *A health-care power of attorney (HCPA) appoints an agent to act for you; a living will does not.*

- *An HCPA applies to all medical decisions unless you specify otherwise; most living wills apply only to a few decisions near the end of your life and are often limited in use if you have a "terminal illness," which has become a slippery term.*

- *An HCPA can include specific instructions to your agent about the issues you care most about or what you want done in particular circumstances.*

If your state doesn't specify a particular form for a living will, Choice in Dying can send you a living will declaration that will keep you from being hooked up to a resuscitation machine. Generally, it must be signed by two witnesses, not including your relatives, heirs, or doctor.

Usually the decision to write a living will should be made after consulting with your doctor and lawyer. If you are writing a living will yourself, it's best to avoid general terms like "extraordinary treatment" in favor of more specific ones like "permanently unconscious."

Living wills are typically either vague ("I don't want to be kept alive if I'm a burden to anyone"—what does that mean?) or so specific as to be inflexible. It's not a problem in drafting them; in the twilight world at the end of life, all lines are blurred, all colors gray. It's simply impossible to predict every possible contingency.

Since living wills are so limited, some lawyers recommend that you have both a living will and an HCPA to handle other kinds of disability or gray-area cases where it's not certain that you're terminally ill or your doctor or state law fail to give your wishes due weight. A living will wouldn't have helped Nancy

WHAT HAPPENS IF I DON'T HAVE A LIVING WILL, HCPA OR HEALTH-CARE DIRECTIVE?

It's likely that life-sustaining treatment will be provided indefinitely even though you will never recover consciousness and will merely be kept alive but unresponsive. Sometimes this can go on for years, with severe emotional consequences for family members. There will also be a financial impact, either for your family or the government. If you don't have an advance directive, someone else may be making the most important decisions of your life—or death. Yet most Americans still don't have advance directives like living wills or HCPAs.

Cruzan, for instance, because she wasn't "terminally ill" and could have lived as long as thirty more years in a persistently vegetative state, but a health-care power of attorney would have permitted a designated person to make the decision to withdraw nutrition and hydration.

Furthermore, the living will form you use may be outdated or otherwise inappropriate under your state's current law (those laws are changing fast). The form will may not address certain questions or, as in the example above, may not conform to your wishes: Do you want all treatment stopped or just artificial respiration? What about provision of food and fluids through an uncomfortable nasogastric tube? It's difficult for any form to address all possible medical issues that may arise when you are unable to communicate your wishes. Better to have a trusted relative or friend make the call.

Finally, despite recent changes in laws, old habits die hard, and many doctors and nurses are still reluctant to turn off life support—even if that's what a patient wants. Surveys show that the medical establishment still routinely overtreats patients with no realistic hope of recovery, ignoring living wills, often angering and tormenting the dying person's loved ones. The most common cases of conflict: removing routine (as distinguished from "heroic") life-sustaining equipment like feeding tubes (as opposed to using them in the first place). That's why you need an advocate appointed by your HCPA to press your intentions.

Even if you're not expected to die in the next few months, if there's no hope that you'll recover consciousness you may want to be allowed to die. But a living will won't force a reluctant doctor to do that; only the agent appointed through your HCPA can demand that step.

Health-Care Advance Directives

The second appendix to this book provides a sample health-care advance directive prepared by AARP, the ABA, and the AMA. It not only permits you to name a health care agent and specify his or her powers (an HCPA), but it also provides instructions about end-of-life treatment (a living will). It also enables you to state in advance whether you want to donate organs at death, and permits you to nominate a guardian of your person should one be required.

Using this comprehensive single document obviously is more convenient and less prone to confusion than having several documents covering portions of your health-care wishes. It meets the legal requirements of most states. Even if it does not meet the requirements of your state, it may provide an effective statement of your wishes if you cannot speak for yourself.

Guardianships and Civil Commitment

The goal of many of the devices described here is to enable you to avoid court-appointed guardianships. The law authorizes courts to appoint guardians (or conservators) for adults adjudicated to be incompetent. These are usually used to protect people experiencing mental illness or retardation, or those who are senile or are addicted to drugs or alcohol. Depending on the law, there can be two kinds of guardians: **guardians of the estate** (often called **conservators**), who are authorized to manage property, and **guardians of the person**, who make medical and personal decisions for the incapacitated person, known as a **ward**. (It's similar to the guardianships set up for children discussed in chapter 6.)

You establish a guardianship by petitioning the court to hold a competency hearing at which testimony (usually medical) is introduced to prove the person can't handle his or her own affairs. If the court agrees, it appoints a guardian (usually the petitioner). The guardianship continues until the ward regains capacity to handle his or her own affairs, which seldom happens, or dies. The ward loses most civil rights, often including the right to make a binding contract, to vote, and to make medical decisions.

A guardian's power varies by the state and court decree; it may be broad or limited. The duties and responsibilities will be enumerated in the appointment document. Usually a bond and inventory will be required and annual reports filed, and the guardian may receive a fee, which is often waived by family members.

Guardianships are relatively clumsy and inefficient ways of taking over decision making for someone else. For example, the guardian must sometimes get the court's permission before spending money or selling assets. Formal notice, a public hearing, or other complicated procedures may be required. You should explore (with a lawyer's advice) the other possibilities listed in this chapter before undertaking one.

If you are afraid someone is seeking a guardianship over you against your wishes, you should see a lawyer. If you agree with the need for guardianship, you can ask the court to appoint the guardian of your choice. As long as there is someone you trust completely, the best protection against involuntary guardianship is to have a health-care advance directive and a durable power of attorney in place before someone tries to impose one on you.

The same goes for commitment to a mental hospital. State laws govern the circumstances under which someone may be involuntarily committed to institutional care. A hearing is required; the standard is whether a person is dangerous to him- or herself or others or can't care for him- or herself. A lawyer is usually appointed to represent the individual whose commitment is sought. If you are committed to an institution, you retain certain rights, and it's likely that after treatment you will be released. If you feel someone is wrongly seeking to have you committed to an institution, see a lawyer immediately.

Organ Donation

The Uniform Anatomical Gift Act, along with similar provisions in most state laws, sets forth your wishes about whether you want your organs donated after your death to other people. Donating your body or other organs to science or medicine has been called the greatest gift, as the thousands of people now on waiting lists to replace their failing organs can attest. You can direct hospitals to donate your organs by filling out a donor card, witnessed by two people, that's often attached to the back of your driver's license. The cards can be obtained at your state's motor vehicles department or by contacting The Living Bank in Houston, telephone 1-800-528-2971; www.livingbank.org. You can also donate organs through a health-care advance directive such as we have provided in this book. Doctors may also ask your family whether they will consent to organ donation on behalf of a terminally ill patient.

AIDS Information

The devastating AIDS epidemic has raised all sorts of legal issues, including those relating to health-care maintenance. Proper estate planning gives people with AIDS (PWAs) a sense of control over their lives and deaths that can help ease the trauma of the disease.

If you have AIDS you need three estate planning documents:

• A general power of attorney, which will give a trusted friend or relative authority to make decisions should you become incompetent or restricted to a hospital or home;

• A health-care power of attorney, which designates someone to make health-care decisions and tells everyone your wishes regarding medical treatment; and

• A will, which disposes of the rest of your property. This is especially important for gay men or women who want to make sure that nonfamily members are provided for.

A will can also provide for a guardianship of any children, which can be important if a family member challenges your wishes for your children. For example, the mother of a person with AIDS might not want his or her surviving partner to bring up a grandchild. However, a guardianship specified in your will can't assure that your wishes are carried out because it's not binding on a court. So an **inter vivos guardianship** (set up in your lifetime) may be better, but that means you may have to give up control of the children before your death. If you anticipate a challenge to a guardianship, it's a good idea to execute an affidavit expressing your desires and stating why other possible guardians are inappropriate. The complexity of such issues make the help of a lawyer essential.

It's vital for a gay person with AIDS to give his or her lawyer a list of family members and be sure the lawyer understands who will and will not inherit property via the will or other estate-planning documents.

A SPECIAL NOTE FOR ELDERLY AMERICANS— AND THEIR CHILDREN

America is getting older. Because of the baby boom and other demographic changes, the number of Americans over age sixty-five will double over the next forty years; 14 million of them will have Alzheimer's disease. By 2050, the elderly will number 67 million, 22 percent of the population. These changes have spawned a whole new legal specialty called "elder law." This book isn't the place to discuss the whole panoply of issues involved, but estate planning makes up a significant component of legal concerns for the elderly.

Most older Americans have small estates, often poorly organized. Too many widowed spouses are left impoverished, often by poor estate planning. Even so, people sixty-five and older hold more than $5 trillion in wealth, and almost a third of Americans are leaving estates worth more than $50,000—double the number thirty years ago. Clearly, many older Americans need to use money management estate-planning devices.

While it sounds cold-blooded to say it, the children of aging

Americans also have a stake in their elders' estate planning, since most of the fruits pass to them.

Most of the protective devices described in this chapter can be especially valuable to elderly Americans. A good estate-planning attorney can advise you on the best mix of them. Good strategies that might benefit older people include:

• **Long-term care insurance.** Medicare pays for only a fraction of nursing home patients. Nursing home insurance can assure a level of funding if worse comes to worst. If you buy it before age sixty-five, the premiums can be relatively affordable. Your children might be able to help you with the payments; after all, every penny saved from insurance increases their inheritance, which might otherwise be drained by nursing home costs.

• **Lifetime gifts.** These are briefly described in chapter 8. It's better not to sell stock to obtain money for cash gifts because if the stock has appreciated since you bought it, you have to pay a tax on the profit when you sell. Better to let the kids inherit the stock because they will inherit it on a "stepped-up" basis (the value when it is inherited) and only have to pay taxes on the increase in value between that time and when the stock is sold. Give the gifts to your child only, not to her and her spouse, because if there's a divorce, she should be able to keep the entire gift as her separate property.

• **Prenuptial or postnuptial agreements.** These are particularly appropriate for second marriages, especially if you or your new spouse have children from previous marriages. See chapter 7 for more.

• **Living trusts.** See the discussion above and in chapter 5.

See chapter 7 for more information on estate planning for the elderly. The most important thing, however, is that you go to an estate or elder-law attorney and plan your estate. Make the hard calls about which children or relatives you want in charge of your health-care decisions, financial arrangements (they may be different people), and so on. Explain to your family why you are designating each relative (and not designating others) for each job—not because you love any of them more than any of the others but because certain people are better for certain jobs. Realize that your children are going to be afraid that, as you age, you might "squander" (in their eyes) their inheritance in Las Vegas or on a new, young spouse or "friend" or on a religious cult or smooth-talking evangelist. Listen to their concerns but explain that you have a right to do with your money what you will.

MEDICAID ESTATE PLANNING

Nursing home costs can be devastating to a family. Planning ahead can make a big difference. Competent Medicaid planning helps an individual who is unable to pay for long-term care properly meet the Medicaid financial eligibility requirements. Planning may also slow the depletion of your estate or preserve some of it for your spouse or dependents.

Medicaid planning usually focuses on families who realistically have no other choice but to rely on Medicaid. Few people would opt for Medicaid if other choices were available, because of disadvantages, including less provider choice, limitations in available care, discrimination against Medicaid recipients, and intrusive involvement of the state in your finances and health care. Medicaid planning uses legally permitted options under Medicaid to preserve assets and try to assure your survivor some financial security.

Unfortunately, most of the self-help advice regarding Medicaid planning is fraught with danger. Even with competent advice tailored to your needs, Medicaid planning is not easy. The goal here is to introduce you to the types of planning strategies and not to provide a do-it-yourself cookbook.

Transfers of assets. Transfers of property for less than full **consideration** (i.e., giving property away in whole or part), except for transfers between spouses, can result in a period of ineligibility for Medicaid benefits. When you apply for Medicaid, you must disclose any transfer made within the last thirty-six months (sixty months for certain transfers involving trusts). Such transfers trigger a period of ineligibility that varies from location to location (see sidebar, below).

Under a new law, effective January 1, 1997, **certain transfers may also be a crime under Federal Medicaid fraud provisions.** If you knowingly dispose of assets to qualify for Medicaid, *and* doing so results in a period of ineligibility for Medicaid, you could face criminal penalties of up to $10,000 in fines and one year in jail. Dubbed the "Granny goes to jail" law, it probably won't be aggressively applied, but it creates considerable anxiety among seniors trying to do legitimate planning. Correct advice and consultation in planning are a must.

One rule of thumb when transferring property for less than full consideration, for purposes of Medicaid planning, is to retain enough assets to be able to pay for nursing home care for the duration of the penalty period. However, this is only a generalization. Every situation is different.

Use of trusts. Irrevocable trusts are another planning tool to help manage the cost of long-term care. Trusts that can be revoked by the creator of the trust are considered countable assets by Medicaid and have no impact on Medicaid eligibility. However, irrevocable trusts, if created at least **sixty months** prior to applying for Medicaid (the "look-back" period for trusts) may help establish Medicaid eligibility while slowing down the depletion of your estate, if the discretion of the trustee to distribute income and principle is sharply limited. Federal law also recognizes certain trusts created for the benefit of persons with disability under sixty-five. Generally, parents who are planning for the long-term care of an adult or disabled child may want to consider this type of trust.

An irrevocable **Miller trust** (named after a legal case) is relevant to persons living in "income cap" states. The problem faced by some persons in these states is that their income may be just over the Medicaid income cap but less than the amount needed to pay privately for a nursing home bed. To remedy this hardship, federal law requires these states to exempt (for purposes of Medicaid eligibility) trusts created for their benefit if the trust is composed only of pension, Social Security, or other income, and if at the individual's death the state is reimbursed by the trust for all Medicaid assistance paid on behalf of the individual. These trusts work by paying out a monthly income just under the Medicaid cap and retaining the rest. The result is that most of the individual's income, supplemented by Medicaid, goes toward payment of the nursing home. The remainder of the person's income remains in the trust until his or her death. The accumulated residue is then paid to Medicaid.

Other limited trust arrangements may be helpful in some cases, but they all require careful assessment and advice and a good dose of caution, and remember that Congress periodically changes the rules, so your strategy may have to change.

Where to Get More Information

We list below a number of organizations that can help you find someone who will work with you on planning your estate.

Also, the probate courts in many states provide forms and sometimes information to the public about how to write and file the documents necessary to estate planning; call yours and see what it has to offer.

For help with living wills and health-care advance directives, you might contact one of the "death with dignity" groups. See below and chapter 12 for more on this.

FINDING LEGAL HELP

- *Finding Legal Help: An Older Person's Guide* is an excellent twenty-page guide produced by Legal Counsel for the Elderly, a program of the American Association of Retired Persons. Send $2.00 to Legal Counsel for the Elderly, P.O. Box 96474, Washington, DC 20090-6474. Telephone, 202-434-2170. Their address on the world wide web is www.aarp.org.

- Sites on the world wide web that enable you to find more information and sometimes even the names of lawyers in your area (in addition to those listed here) include www.seniorlaw.com and www.netplanning.com.

- The American Bar Association's Section of Real Property, Probate and Trust Law offers a free directory of members who serve on its

181

committees. Many practice estate planning, estate and trust administration, and disability planning. The directory of members gives you the names of thousands of attorneys, and committee memberships help highlight their interests and expertise. Write the section at American Bar Association, 750 N. Lake Shore Drive, mail stop 7.1, Chicago, IL 60611, or call 312-988-5590. You can also find out more information about the section in the ABA's home page on the world wide web at www.abanet.org.

- The American College of Trust and Estate Counsel offers a membership listing of lawyers by state whose practices concentrate in estate planning. To obtain a listing for your state, write to ACTEC at 3415 S. Sepulveda Blvd., Suite 330, Los Angeles, CA 90034. Telephone, 310-398-1888; fax, 310-572-7280. Their home page on the world wide web is www.actec.org.

- National Association of Estate Planners and Councils can provide a listing of attorneys certified in estate planning through experience, education, and examination. (However, be aware that many estate planning specialists have not sought certification and so are not listed.) Call or write the association at 270 South Bryn Mawr Ave., P.O. Box 46, Bryn Mawr, PA 19010-2196. Telephone, 610-526-1389; fax, 610-526-1224; home page, www.naepc.org.

- The National Academy of Elder Law Attorneys (NAELA) publishes a directory of elder law attorney members, including those certified in elder law by the National Elder Law Foundation. (The specialty is new, and many lawyers qualified in elder law have not sought certification.) NAELA also provides consumer publications for older persons and their families. NAELA is at 1604 N. Country Club, Tucson, AZ 85716. Telephone, 520-881-4005; fax, 520-325-7925; home page on the world wide web, www.naela.org.

- Local bar associations often operate lawyer referral services. You'll find one close to you through www.abanet.org/referral/home.html.

- State bar associations can provide information about lawyer discipline and complaint procedures should you have a serious complaint about your attorney. You can also get a complete listing of lawyer disciplinary agencies by accessing www.abanet.org/cpr/disciplinary.html.

- Your local area agency on aging should be able to inform you about the availability of free or reduced-fee legal assistance available to persons over sixty in your community. Look in your local government listings under "aging" or call the National Eldercare Locator at 1-800-677-1116 to find the agency on aging nearest you. You can also search the data base of the National Eldercare Locator online through their web site at www.aoa.dhhs.gov/elderpage/locator.html.

- Some states—including Arizona, California, Florida, Louisiana, New Mexico, North Carolina, South Carolina, and Texas—certify lawyers in the specialty area of estate planning. Contact the following organizations in these states to find lists of lawyers certified as specialists in this field.

State Bar of Arizona Board of Legal Specialization and MCLE
Lisa Ricchiuti-Casas, Administrator
101 West Monroe, Suite 1800
Phoenix, AZ 85003-1742
Phone: (602) 340-7327
Internet: www.azbar.org/FindingLawyer/bls.asp

State Bar of California Office of Certification
Phyllis J. Culp, Director
180 Howard Street
San Francisco, CA 94105
Phone: (415) 538-2118
Internet: www.calbar.org/lgl-spec.htm

Florida Bar Board of Legal Specialization and Education
Dawna G. Bicknell, Executive Director
650 Appalachee Parkway
Tallahassee, FL 32399-2300
Phone: (904) 561-5655
Internet: www.flabar.org

Louisiana Board of Legal Specialization
Catherine S. Zulli, Executive Director
601 St. Charles Avenue

New Orleans, LA 70130
Phone: (504) 566-1600
Internet: www./lsba.org/html/lawyer_specialization.html

New Mexico Board of Legal Specialization
Ingrid Mulvey, Administrator—Court Regulated Programs
P.O. Box 25883
Albuquerque, NM 87125
Phone: (505) 797-6056
Internet: www.nmbar.org/statebar/courtregprograms/
   legspecrules.htm

North Carolina Board of Legal Specialization
Alice Neece Moseley, Executive Director
P.O. Box 25908
Raleigh, NC 27611
Phone: (919) 828-4620

South Carolina Supreme Court Commission on CLE and Specialization
Harold L. Miller, Executive Director
P.O. Box 2138
Columbia, SC 29202
Phone: (803) 799-5578
Internet: www.commcle.org

Texas Board of Legal Specialization
Gary W. McNeil, Executive Director
400 West 15th Street, Suite 1540
Austin, TX 78711
Phone: (512) 463-1454 or 1-800-204-222, ext. 1454
Internet: www.tbls.org

APPENDIX A

■

Estate-Planning Checklist

This initial estate-planning questionnaire is presented in a narrative form. The detailed explanations and the space provided for answers are designed to garner more complete and helpful information than would be afforded by merely filling in blanks.

ESTATE PLANNING REVIEW FOR

_____

The Purpose of This Questionnaire

Your lawyer will use the information you provide in this questionnaire:

1. To help you organize personal and financial information so that you can assess your current estate plans and evaluate whether changes are desired or required.

2. To provide your estate planning attorney with the information needed to make a similar analysis.

3. To help you evaluate your lawyer's estate-planning recommendations. The estate plan is your plan, not your lawyer's, and you must be satisfied that it is workable.

The information you provide must be as accurate and complete as possible. If you are uncertain about exact information, tell your lawyer that and give your best assessment. If your lawyer believes that exact information is required, he or she will ask you to be more precise.

We recognize that this questionnaire is a fairly intrusive document. Keep in mind, however, that the more complete the information is, the better it will equip you and your lawyer throughout the planning process to come up with the best possible estate-planning alternatives. Your information will be kept confidential by your lawyer unless you authorize or request its release to others.

PERSONAL AND FAMILY INFORMATION

State the names requested below exactly as you want them to appear in your will and other estate-planning documents. Where the space on the form is insufficient, please use extra sheets of paper.

Your name: _____

Date of birth: _____

Spouse's name: _____

Date of birth: _____

Home address: _____

Telephone no.: _____

Are you a United States citizen? _____

If not, of what country are you a citizen? _____

Is your spouse a citizen of the United States? _____

If not, of what country is he/she a citizen? _____

Your Children, Their Spouses, and Their Children

Indicate which, if any, of your children is your child but not your spouse's or vice versa. Also, show the date and place of adoption of any adopted child. Be sure to include any deceased child and indicate the date of the child's death and his or her surviving spouse and children.

1. (a) Child: _____ Date of birth: _____

   (b) Personal data (specify if the child is from a prior marriage, adopted, deceased, etc.): _____

   _____

   (c) Child's spouse: _____

   (d) Child's children (and their dates of birth): _____

   _____

   _____

   _____

2. (a) Child: _____ Date of birth: _____

   (b) Personal data (specify if the child is from a prior marriage, adopted, deceased, etc.): _____

   _____

   (c) Child's spouse: _____

   (d) Child's children (and their dates of birth): _____

   _____

   _____

   _____

3. (a) Child: _____ Date of birth: _____

   (b) Personal data (specify if the child is from a prior marriage, adopted, deceased, etc.): _____

   _____

   (c) Child's spouse: _____

   (d) Child's children (and their dates of birth): _____

   _____

   _____

   _____

4. If either you or your spouse has been married previously, state the name of each prior spouse and indicate whether he or she is now living (if living, give his or her address):_____

_____

_____

If either you or your spouse has been divorced, attach a copy of the divorce decree.

5. Is there other important personal information that might affect your estate plans? For example, does a member of your family have a serious long-term medical or physical problem that will require special care or attention in the future? _____

_____

_____

PERSONAL AND FAMILY FINANCIAL ASSETS

In the following section, please provide as much detail as you can about assets, such as addresses and account numbers. For property interests, such as real estate, detail will be helpful, including copies of deeds. With regard to real estate, it is important for your lawyer to know the location (city and state) of the property, how the title is held, and the character of the property: that is, residence (condominium or co-op), shopping center, apartment house, or similar description.

The following abbreviations may be used to describe certain attributes of particular assets:

JT   = Joint tenancy with right of survivorship
TE   = Tenancy by the entirety
TC   = Tenancy in common
H   = Husband's name alone
W   = Wife's name alone
LT   = Land trust
FMV = Fair market value (or your best estimate)

CV = Cash value of life insurance policy
PV = Proceeds of life insurance policy

1. Personal residence:

   Address: _____

   Description (e.g., single family, condo, co-op, or similar description):

   _____

   _____

   How you hold title: _____

   Mortgage holder (name and address): _____

   _____

   FMV: _____ Mortgage balance, if any: _____

   Mortgage life insurance? _____

2. Other personal residences or vacation homes:

   Address: _____

   Description: _____

   How you hold title: _____

   Mortgage holder (name and address): _____

   _____

   FMV: _____ Mortgage balance, if any: _____

   Mortgage life insurance? _____

3. Personal and household effects: If you think that the general categories do not provide an adequate description, please provide additional detail. Also, state your best estimate of the value of each kind of property and who owns it (how you hold title).

   Automobiles (make, year, value, lien): _____

   _____

   _____

General personal and household effects such as furniture, furnishings, books, and pictures of no special value:

_____

Valuable jewelry (indicate if insured; if so, for how much and by which company, including policy number): _____

_____

_____

Valuable works of art (indicate if insured; if so, for how much and by which company, including policy number): _____

_____

_____

Valuable antiques (indicate if insured; if so, for how much and by which company, including policy number): _____

_____

_____

Other valuable collections (e.g., coins, stamps, gold) (indicate if insured; if so, for how much and by which company, including policy number):

_____

_____

_____

Other tangible personal property that does not seem to be covered by any of the other categories: _____

_____

_____

_____

4. Cash, cash deposits, and cash equivalents: State the account number and the name and address of each bank or institution and who owns each item.

(a) Checking accounts, including money market accounts.

You: _____

_____

Spouse: _____

_____

Jointly with _____: _____

_____

(b) Ordinary savings accounts.

You: _____

_____

Spouse: _____

_____

Jointly with _____: _____

_____

(c) Certificates of deposit.

You: _____

_____

Spouse: _____

_____

Jointly with _____: _____

_____

(d) Short-term U.S. obligations (T-bills).

You: _____

_____

Spouse: _____

_____

Jointly with _____: _____

_____

5. Pension and profit-sharing plans, IRAs, ESOPs, or other tax-favored employee benefits plans.

(a) Pension plans. Indicate name and address of plan administrator.

You: _____

Vested: _____ Value: _____

Spouse: _____

Vested: _____ Value: _____

(b) Profit-sharing plans. Indicate name and address of plan administrator.

You: _____

Vested: _____ Value: _____

Spouse: _____

Vested: _____ Value: _____

(c) Individual Retirement Accounts (IRAs). Indicate account number and name and address of bank or broker.

You: _____

Value: _____

Spouse: _____

Value: _____

(d) Other tax-qualified employee benefits plan interests. Please provide similar information. _____

_____

_____

6. Life insurance on your life.

(a) Ordinary life insurance. List company, name, address, and policy number. _____

_____

Face amount of policies (proceeds): _____

If you do not own it, who does? _____

Beneficiaries: _____

_____

Cash value: _____ Loans, if any, against it: _____

Amount of accidental death benefits, if any: _____

(b) Term/group term insurance. List company, name, address, and policy number. _____

_____

Face amount of policies:_____

Owner other than you: _____

Beneficiaries: _____

_____

Cash value: _____ Loans, if any, against it: _____

Accidental death benefits: _____

_____

(c) Please supply similar information with respect to other life insurance or other insurance having life insurance features:

_____

_____

_____

7. (a) Life insurance on your spouse's life. List company name, address, and policy number. _____

_____

_____

Face amount of ordinary life insurance: _____

Owner other than spouse: _____

Beneficiaries: _____

_____

Cash value: _____ Loans, if any, against it: _____

Accidental death benefits: _____

(b) Term/group term life insurance (list company name, address, etc.): _____

_____

Face amount of term insurance: _____

Owner other than spouse: _____

Beneficiaries: _____

_____

Cash value: _____ Loans, if any, against it: _____

Accidental death benefits: _____

(c) Other insurance on spouse's life: _____

_____

_____

8. Closely held business interests. Describe any interest you have in a family or other business with limited shareholders. Include the nature of the business, its form of organization (e.g., corporation, partnership, and the like), whether you are active in its operations, and your estimate of its value. If it is a corporation, please indicate whether an "S election" is in force with respect to the federal taxation of the corporation. _____

_____

_____

_____

With respect to any such business, do you believe it would continue to operate successfully in the event of your permanent absence from it or the permanent absence of some other key person?

_____

_____

9. Investment assets. With respect to each category, please state the owner (how title is held) and the approximate value. Please list name of broker and number of account.

(a) Publicly traded stocks and corporate bonds.

You: _____

Spouse: _____

Jointly owned with _____: _____

_____

(b) Municipal bonds.

You: _____

Spouse: _____

Jointly owned with _____: _____

_____

(c) Long-term U.S. Treasury Notes and Bonds.

You: _____

Spouse: _____

Jointly owned with _____: _____

_____

(d) Limited partnership interests.

You: _____

Spouse: _____

Jointly owned with _____: _____

_____

(e) Other investments. Please describe the general nature and value of other investment interests.

You: _____

Spouse: _____

Jointly owned with _____: _____

Other Interests of Current or Future Value

1. Interests in trusts. Describe any trusts created by you, by any other person, such as a parent or ancestor, in which you or a member of your immediate family has a right to receive distributions of income or principal, whether such distributions are actually being received or anticipated in the future. Be as specific as you can. If possible, submit a copy of the trust agreement. If the trust agreement is not available, show the date the trust was created, whether it can be amended or revoked, whether someone has a power of appointment over it, when the trust terminates, and who will receive the trust property upon termination. Also, state the approximate current value of the trust and the annual income from it.

_____

_____

_____

_____

_____

2. Anticipated inheritances. If you or any other members of your immediate family are likely to receive substantial inheritances in the foreseeable future from persons other than yourself or your spouse, describe your best estimate of the value and the nature of each inheritance. _____

_____

_____

_____

3. Other assets or interests of value. Describe the general nature, form of ownership, and your estimate of the value of any asset or interest of value that does not seem to fit in any of the categories above. _____

_____

_____

Liabilities

Describe here substantial financial liabilities not reflected in the asset information you have provided above. If they are secured, indicate the nature of the security. Also, show any substantial contingent liabilities, such as personal guarantees you have made on obligations of a business, a family member, or any other person. Indicate whether you have insured against any of these obligations in the event of your death or if the obligations do not survive your death. _____

_____

_____

_____

_____

_____

PERSONAL ESTATE-PLANNING OBJECTIVES

1. How would you dispose of your estate at your death if there were no such thing as estate or inheritance taxes? _____

_____

_____

2. In the event of your death, would your spouse or children be likely to receive income from sources other than your estate, such as the continuance or resumption by your spouse of his or her vocation or profession? _____

_____

_____

3. Describe any personal objectives you have for your family and your estate that override possible adverse tax consequences arising from trying to achieve them. _____

_____

_____

_____

_____

GUARDIANS, EXECUTORS, AND TRUSTEES

1. Guardians for minor children. If you have minor children, you may designate in your will a guardian or guardians of the person and the estate in the event of your death and/or your spouse's.

   (a) Guardian(s) of the person.

   Name(s): _____

   _____

   _____

   Address(es): _____

   _____

   _____

   (b) Successor guardian(s) of the person.

   Name(s): _____

   _____

   _____

Address(es): _____

_____

_____

(c) Guardian(s) of the estate, if different.

Name(s): _____

_____

_____

Address(es): _____

_____

_____

(d) Successor guardian(s) of the estate.

Name(s): _____

_____

_____

Address(es): _____

_____

_____

2. Executor. Your executor has the responsibility to wind up your affairs at your death, see to it that your assets are collected, that claims,
expenses, and estate and inheritance taxes are paid, and then distribute your property to trustees or others you have named. It is a
task of limited duration, substantial responsibility, and much work.

(a) Principal executor(s).

Name(s): _____

_____

_____

Address(es): _____

_____

_____

(b) Successor executor(s).

Name(s): _____

_____

_____

Address(es): _____

_____

_____

3. Trustees. Your trustees have the responsibility for the long-range management of property that is to be held in trust for the benefit of the beneficiaries of trusts you may create.

Depending on the terms of the trust, there may be adverse tax consequences if a trustee has an interest or possible interest in the trust, although usually if the trustee's discretion is limited those adverse tax consequences are similarly limited. A trustee can be a corporation (qualified to act) or an individual. You may choose to have co-trustees, one of which may or may not be a corporation. Because corporate trustees must charge fees for their services, they may decline to accept small trusts. Their fees to administer a small trust may turn out to be disproportionately large if they are to cover their costs in handling the trust.

In general, choose a trustee with the following qualities: integrity, mature judgment, fiscal responsibility, and reasonable business and investment acumen. If you wish to select co-trustees, you may want to choose them for how well their individual strengths complement each other. Frequently, the same person(s) or corporation selected as executor(s) may be designated as trustee(s).

(a) Principal trustee(s).

Name(s): _____

_____

_____

Address(es): _____

_____

_____

(b) Substitute trustee(s) (to act if one or more of the principal trustees cannot or will not act).

Name(s): _____

_____

_____

Address(es): _____

_____

_____

OTHER MATTERS

1. Other factors. Describe or list here any facts or matters that do not seem to be covered by the other sections of this questionnaire and that you believe may be important for your estate-planning attorney to know. _____

_____

_____

_____

_____

2. Community property. If you now live in or have lived in one of the states listed below, or if you own real estate in one of these states, please circle the name of the state, provide a description of the property and a copy of the deed, and indicate whether you and your spouse have entered into any agreement about whether that property is separate property.
States: Arizona, California, Idaho, Louisiana, Nevada, New Mexico, Texas, Washington, Wisconsin

_____

_____

_____

_____

3. Powers of attorney. Have you given a power of attorney to your spouse, a child, or any other person authorizing him or her to do either specific things on your behalf or to act generally on your behalf? If so, please indicate to whom it was given, the nature of the power (specific or general), the date, and the location of the document granting the power. _____

_____

_____

_____

4. Living will. Have you signed any document indicating your wishes concerning "heroic" or extraordinary measures to save your life in the event of a catastrophic illness or injury? _____ If not, would you like to do so? _____

5. Health-care power. Have you signed any document specifically authorizing another person such as your spouse to make decisions with respect to your health care in the event that you are unable to do so? _____ If not, would you like to do so? _____

Date completed: _____

APPENDIX B

■

Health Care Advance Directive

CAUTION: This Health Care Advance Directive is a general form provided for your convenience. While it meets the legal requirements of most states, it may or may not fit the requirements or your particular state. Many states have special forms or special procedures for creating Health Care Advance Directives. If your state's law does not clearly recognize this document, it may still provide an effective statement of your wishes if you cannot speak for yourself. The directions for filling out the form are given first, followed by the form itself on page 208.

Section 1. Health Care Agent

Print your full name in this spot as the principal or creator of the health care advance directive.

Print the full name, address and telephone number of the person (age 18 or older) you appoint as your health care agent. Appoint *only* a person with whom you have talked and whom you trust to understand and carry out your values and wishes.

Many states limit the persons who can serve as your agent. If you want to meet all existing state restrictions, *do not* name any of the following as your agent, since some states will not let them act in that role:

■ your health care providers, including physicians;

■ staff of health care facilities or nursing care facilities providing your care;

- guardians of your finances (also called conservators);
- employees of government agencies financially responsible for your care;
- any person serving as agent for 10 or more persons.

Section 2. Alternate Agents

It is a good idea to name alternate agents in case your first agent is not available. Of course, only appoint alternates if you fully trust them to act faithfully as your agent and you have talked to them about serving as your agent. Print the appropriate information in this section. You can name as many alternate agents as you wish, but place them in the order you wish them to serve.

Section 3. Effective Date and Durability

This sample document is effective if and when you cannot make health care decisions. Your agent and your doctor determine if you are in this condition. Some state laws include specific procedures for determining your decision-making ability. If you wish, you can include other effective dates or other criteria for determining that you cannot make health care decisions (such as requiring two physicians to evaluate your decision-making ability). You also can state that the power will end at some later date or event before death.

In any case, you have the *right to revoke* or take away the agent's authority at any time. To revoke, notify your agent or health care provider orally or in writing. If you revoke, it is best to notify in writing both your agent and physician and anyone else who has a copy of the directive. Also destroy the health care advance directive document itself.

Section 4. Agent's Powers

This grant of power is intended to be as broad as possible. Unless you set limits, your agent will have authority to make any decision you could make to consent to or stop any type of health care.

This appendix is adapted from the booklet "Shape Your Health-Care Future with Health-Care Advance Directives."

Even under this broad grant of authority, your agent still must follow your wishes and directions, communicated by you in any manner now or in the future.

To specifically limit or direct your agent's power, you must complete Part II of the advance directive, section 6, on page 212.

Section 5. My Instructions About End-of-Life Treatment

The subject of end-of-life treatment is particularly important to many people. In this section, you can give general or specific instructions on the subject. The different paragraphs are options—*choose only one*, or write your desires or instructions in your own words (in the last option). If you are satisfied with your agent's knowledge of your values and wishes and you do not want to include instructions in the form, initial the first option and do not give instructions in the form.

Any instructions you give here will guide your agent. If you do not appoint an agent, they will guide any health care providers or surrogate decisionmakers who must make a decision for you if you cannot do so yourself. The instruction choices in the form describe different treatment goals you may prefer, depending on your condition.

Directive in Your Own Words. If you would like to state your wishes about end-of-life treatment in your own words instead of choosing one of the options provided you can do so in this section. Since people sometimes have different opinions on whether nutrition and hydration should be refused or stopped under certain circumstances, be sure to address this issue clearly in your directive. Nutrition and hydration means food and fluids given through a nasogastric tube or tube into your stomach, intestines, or veins, and *does not include* non-intrusive methods such as spoon feeding or moistening of lips and mouth.

Some states allow the stopping of nutrition and hydration only if you expressly authorize it. If you are creating your own directive, and you do not want nutrition and hydration, state so clearly.

Section 6. Any Other Health Care Instructions or Limitations or Modifications of my Agent's Powers

In this section, you can provide instructions about other health care issues that are not end-of-life treatment or nutrition and hydration. For example, you might want to include your wishes about issues like non-emergency surgery, elective medical treatments or admission to a nursing home. Again, be careful in these instructions not to place limitations on your agent that you do not intend. For example, while you may not want to be admitted to a nursing home, placing such a restriction may make things impossible for your agent if other options are not available.

You also may limit your agent's powers in any way you wish. For example, you can instruct your agent to refuse any specific types of treatment that are against your religious beliefs or unacceptable to you for any other reasons. These might include blood transfusions, electro-convulsive therapy, sterilization, abortion, amputation, psychosurgery, or admission to a mental institution, etc. Some states limit your agent's authority to consent to or refuse some of these procedures, regardless of your health care advance directive.

Be very careful about stating limitations, because the specific circumstances surrounding future health care decisions are impossible to predict. If you do not want any limitations, simply write in *"No limitations."*

Section 7. Protection of Third Parties Who Rely on My Agent

In most states, health care providers cannot be forced to follow the directions of your agent if they object. However most states also require providers to help transfer you to another provider who is willing to honor your instructions. To encourage compliance with the health care advance directive, this paragraph states that providers who rely in good faith on the agent's statements and decisions will not be held civilly liable for their actions.

Section 8. Donations of Organs at Death

In this section you can state your intention to donate bodily organs and tissues at death. If you do not wish to be an organ donor, initial the first option. The second option is a donation of any or all organs or parts. The third option allows you to donate only those organs or tissues you specify. Consider mentioning the heart, liver, lung, kidney, pancreas, intestine, cornea, bone, skin, heart valves, tendons, ligaments and saphenous vein. Finally, you may limit the use of your organs by *crossing out* any of the four purposes listed that you do not want (transplant, therapy, research or education). If you do not cross out any of these options, your organs may be used for any of these purposes.

Section 9. Nomination of Guardian

Appointing a health care agent helps to avoid a court-appointed guardian for health care decision-making. However, if a court becomes involved for any reason, this paragraph expressly names your agent to serve as guardian. A court does not have to follow your nomination, but normally it will honor your wishes unless there is good reason to override your choice.

Section 10. Administrative Provisions

These items address miscellaneous matters that could affect the implementation of your health care advance directive.

Signing the Document

Required state procedures for signing this kind of document vary. Some require only a signature, while others have very detailed witnessing requirements. Some states simply require notarization.

The procedure in this book is likely to be far more complex than your state law requires because it combines the formal requirements from virtually every state. Follow it if you do not know your state's requirements and you want to meet the signature requirements of virtually every state.

First, sign and date the document in the presence of two witnesses and a notary. Your witnesses should know your identity personally and be able to declare that you appear to be of sound mind and under no duress or undue influence.

In order to meet the different witnessing requirements of most states, do *not* have the following people witness your signature:

- Anyone you have chosen to make health care decisions on your behalf (agent or alternate agents).
- Your treating physician, health care provider, health facility operator, or an employee of any of these.
- Insurers or employees of your life/health insurance provider.
- Anyone financially responsible for your health care costs.
- Anyone related to you by blood, marriage, or adoption.
- Anyone entitled to any part of your estate under an existing will or by operation of law or anyone who will benefit financially from your death. Your creditors should not serve as witnesses.

If you are in a nursing home or other institution, a few states have additional witnessing requirements. This form does not include witnessing language for this situation. Contact a patient advocate or an ombudsman to find out about the state's requirements in these cases.

Second, have your signature notarized. Some states permit notarization as an alternative to witnessing. Doing both witnessing and notarization is more than most states require, but doing both will meet the execution requirements of most states. This form includes a typical notary statement, but it is wise to check state law in case it requires a special form of notary acknowledgement.

PART I APPOINTMENT OF HEALTH CARE AGENT

1. Health Care Agent

I, _____ hereby appoint
PRINCIPAL

_____
AGENT'S NAME

_____
ADDRESS

( ) _____   ( ) _____
HOME PHONE #   WORK PHONE #

as my agent to make health and personal care decisions for me as authorized in this document.

2. Alternate Agents

If

- I revoke my Agent's authority; or
- my Agent becomes unwilling or unavailable to act; or
- if my agent is my spouse and I become legally separated or divorced,

I name the following (each to act alone and successively, in the order named) as alternates to my Agent:

A. First Alternate Agent _____

   Address _____

   Telephone _____

B. Second Alternate Agent _____

   Address _____

   Telephone _____

3. Effective Date and Durability

By this document I intend to create a health care advance directive. It is effective upon, and only during, any period in which I cannot make or communicate a choice regarding a particular health care decision. My agent, attending physician and any other necessary experts should determine that I am unable to make choices about health care.

4. Agent's Powers

I give my Agent full authority to make health care decisions for me. My Agent shall follow my wishes as known to my Agent either through this document or through other means. In interpreting my wishes, I intend my Agent's authority to be as broad as possible, except for any limitations I state in this form. In making any decision, my Agent shall try to discuss the proposed decision with me to determine my desires if I am able to communicate in any way. If my Agent cannot determine the choice I would want, then my Agent shall make a choice for me based upon what my Agent believes to be in my best interests.

Unless specifically limited by Section 6, below, my Agent is authorized as follows:

A. To consent, refuse, or withdraw consent to any and all types of health care. Health care means any care, treatment, service or procedure to maintain, diagnose or otherwise affect an individual's physical or mental condition. It includes, but is not limited to, artificial respiration, nutritional support and hydration, medication and cardiopulmonary resuscitation;

B. To have access to medical records and information to the same extent that I am entitled, including the right to disclose the contents to others as appropriate for my health care;

C. To authorize my admission to or discharge (even against medical advice) from any hospital, nursing home, residential care, assisted living or similar facility or service;

D. To contract on my behalf for any health care related service or facility on my behalf, without my Agent incurring personal financial liability for such contracts;

E. To hire and fire medical, social service, and other support personnel responsible for my care;

F. To authorize, or refuse to authorize, any medication or procedure intended to relieve pain, even though such use may lead to physical damage, addiction, or hasten the moment of (but not intentionally cause) my death;

G. To make anatomical gifts of part or all of my body for medical purposes, authorize an autopsy, and direct the disposition of my remains, to the extent permitted by law;

H. To take any other action necessary to do what I authorize here, including (but not limited to) granting any waiver or release from liability required by any hospital, physician, or other health care provider; signing any documents relating to refusals of treatment or the leaving of a facility against medical advice; and pursuing any legal action in my name at the expense of my estate to force compliance with my wishes as determined by my Agent, or to seek actual or punitive damages for the failure to comply.

PART II INSTRUCTIONS ABOUT HEALTH CARE

5. My Instructions About End-of-Life Treatment

(Initial only ONE of the following statements)

_____ **NO SPECIFIC INSTRUCTIONS.** My agent knows my values and wishes, so I do not wish to include any specific instructions here.

_____ **DIRECTIVE TO WITHHOLD OR WITHDRAW TREATMENT.** Although I greatly value life, I also believe that at some point, life has such diminished value that medical treatment should be stopped, and I should be allowed to die. Therefore, I do not want to receive treatment, including nutrition and hydration, when the treatment will not give me a meaningful quality of life. I do not want my life prolonged . . .

_____ . . . if the treatment will leave me in a condition of permanent unconsciousness, such as with an irreversible coma or a persistent vegetative state.

_____ . . . if the treatment will leave me with some consciousness but in an irreversible condition of complete, or nearly complete, loss of ability to think or communicate with others.

_____ . . . if the treatment will leave me with some ability to think or communicate with others, but the likely risks and burdens of treatment outweigh the expected benefits. Risks, burdens and benefits include consideration of length of life, quality of life, financial costs, and my personal dignity and privacy.

_____ **DIRECTIVE TO RECEIVE TREATMENT.** I want my life to be prolonged as long as possible, no matter what my quality of life.

_____ **DIRECTIVE ABOUT END-OF-LIFE TREATMENT IN MY OWN WORDS:**

_____

_____

_____

_____

_____

6. Any Other Health Care Instructions or Limitations or Modifications of my Agent's Powers

_____

_____

_____

_____

_____

7. Protection of Third Parties Who Rely on My Agent

No person who relies in good faith upon any representations by my Agent or Alternate Agent(s) shall be liable to me, my estate, my heirs or assigns, for recognizing the Agent's authority.

8. Donations of Organs at Death

Upon my death:
(Initial one)

_____ I do *not* wish to donate any organs or tissues, OR

_____ I give *any* needed organs, tissues, or parts, OR

_____ I give *only* the following organs, tissues, or parts: *(please specify)*

_____

_____

My gift (if any) is for the following purposes:
(Cross out any of the following you do not want)

- ■ Transplant
- ■ Research
- ■ Therapy
- ■ Education

9. Nomination of Guardian

If a guardian of my person should for any reason need to be appointed, I nominate my Agent (or his or her alternate then authorized to act), named above.

10. Administrative Provisions

(All apply)

- ■ I revoke any prior health care advance directive.
- ■ This health care advance directive is intended to be valid in any jurisdiction in which it is presented.
- ■ A copy of this advance directive is intended to have the same effect as the original.

Signing the Document

BY SIGNING HERE I INDICATE THAT I UNDERSTAND THE CONTENTS OF THIS DOCUMENT AND THE EFFECT OF THIS GRANT OF POWERS TO MY AGENT.

I sign my name to this Health Care Advance Directive on this

_____ day of _____ , 19_____ .

My Signature _____

My Name _____

My current home address is _____

_____

_____

Witness Statement

I declare that the person who signed or acknowledged this document is personally known to me, that he/she signed or acknowledged this health care advance directive in my presence, and that he/she appears to be of sound mind and under no duress, fraud, or undue influence.

I am not:

- the person appointed as agent by this document,
- the patient's health care provider,
- an employee of the patient's health care provider,
- financially responsible for the person's health care,
- related to the principal by blood, marriage, or adoption, and,
- to the best of my knowledge, a creditor of the principal/or entitled to any part of his/her estate under a will now existing or by operation of law.

Witness #1:

_____

SIGNATURE   DATE

_____

PRINT NAME

_____

TELEPHONE

_____

RESIDENT ADDRESS

Witness #2:

_____

SIGNATURE   DATE

_____

PRINT NAME

_____

TELEPHONE

_____

RESIDENT ADDRESS

Notarization

STATE OF _____.)   My Commission Expires:

) ss.

COUNTY OF _____.)

On this ____ day of _____, 19___,

the said, _____   _____

known to me (or satisfactorily proven) to   NOTARY PUBLIC
be the person named in the foregoing instrument, personally appeared before me,
a Notary Public, within and for the State
and County aforesaid, and acknowledged
that he or she freely and voluntarily executed the same for the purposes stated
therein.

INDEX